Advance Praise for *Identity Safe Spaces at Home and School*

"This compelling book combines up-to-date research with portraits of students, parents, and educators who share ways to foster positive identity development and achievement. The authors provide tools to engage families in cultivating student diversity as an asset and strength-based practices for promoting equity, agency, compassion, and belonging at home and at school. This book provides a valuable blueprint for school teams and family engagement partnerships focused on equity."
—**Linda Darling-Hammond**, president, Learning Policy Institute
and professor emeritus, Stanford University

"This exciting, bold book explains why identity safety matters for all students and the implications for home–school collaboration. Information and activities help us look within ourselves to explore our own identities and our own implicit and explicit biases. There are great tools to consider for building agency and resiliency, which move away from the 'same old habits' by offering professional growth tools for evaluating, strengthening, and celebrating home–school partnerships. In essence, this is a book that combines empowering knowledge and practice to enact important identity safe spaces for everyone at school."
—**Margarita Espino Calderón**, professor emerita,
Johns Hopkins University

"The publication of this seminal text comes not a day too early. Cohn-Vargas and Zacarian offer up a multitude of proactive interventions to support all K–12 kids. My graduate students in Educational Leadership will be required to read every important, research-based page."
—**Donald Cox**, professor, Notre Dame de
Namur University, Belmont, CA

"Cohn-Vargas and Zacarian extend previous literature advocating identity safety in classrooms to foreground how partnerships between home and school can help foster unique identities in young people. The fundamental importance of identity, and how it can develop in caring cultures, are explored in both theoretical and practical terms. This book is essential reading for communities that value diversity as a means to equity and strive actively to empower their youth with pride in personal identity."
—**Penelope Watson**, honorary academic,
University of Auckland

"How can a multidiverse population of students be made to feel emotionally safe enough to prosper from the education they are offered? In their text Identity Safe Spaces at Home and School, Becki Cohn-Vargas and Debbie

T0373393

Zacarian answer this question, so relevant today, with research-supported practical ideas. Appropriate for college courses as well as professional development experiences, this much-needed resource for K–12 educators and administrators describes how to design identify safe practices that support students at school and how to partner with families to extend a sense of well-being at home."

—**Diane Lapp**, Distinguished Professor of Education,
San Diego State University

"I highly recommend this book, with deep gratitude to the authors and the courageous contributors who shared their stories. This book comes at a time when many of our children and youth are vulnerable on multiple levels in their schools and communities. Every educator and education leader who is committed to creating identity safe environments, where all learners can enter being fully themselves and reach their potential, will find in this volume inspiration, a firm theoretical and research foundation, and clear action steps to take in support of affirming multidiverse students. Thank you!"

—**Cristina Sánchez-López**, Paridad Education Consulting

"Becki Cohn-Vargas and Debbie Zacarian don't just tell us how to build identity safe spaces that challenge inequality; they show us through research, practice, and lived experience. Many families and educators struggle with knowing what to do and how to do it, and these experts give us practical tools and strategies that can be used to change lives today."

—**Mary C. Murphy**, Class of 1948 Herman B Wells
Endowed Professor, Indiana University

"It has never been more important than now to create identity safe spaces both at school and at home. Becki Cohn-Vargas and Debbie Zacarian's new book recognizes this urgency and offers a powerful, comprehensive approach to achieve it."

—**Andrea Honigsfeld**, professor, TESOL Program, Molloy College

"It's never been more important to make schools and classrooms genuine places of belonging for all kids and all families. But how do you do it? Becki Cohn-Vargas and Debbie Zacarian show how educators can welcome every child and their whole self to school. If you want to make every kid's identity an asset in school, this is the place to start."

—**Greg Walton**, professor of psychology, Stanford University

Identity Safe Spaces at Home and School

Partnering to Overcome Inequity

Becki Cohn-Vargas and Debbie Zacarian

Foreword by Claude Steele

TEACHERS COLLEGE PRESS

TEACHERS COLLEGE | COLUMBIA UNIVERSITY
NEW YORK AND LONDON

Published by Teachers College Press,® 1234 Amsterdam Avenue, New York, NY 10027

Front cover by Holly Grundon / BHG Graphics. Image by Phil Sheldon / Unsplash.

Library of Congress Cataloging-in-Publication Data is available at loc.gov

ISBN 978-0-8077-6922-5 (paper)
ISBN 978-0-8077-6923-2 (hardcover)
ISBN 978-0-8077-8215-6 (ebook)

Printed on acid-free paper
Manufactured in the United States of America

This book is a result of the unwavering support from our loving families,
individuals who generously shared their personal stories with us,
and the incredible students and families we've had the privilege to
serve throughout our careers. To all of you, we dedicate this book
with profound gratitude and wholehearted appreciation.

Contents

Foreword

Over the past decades, I've been researching, writing, and presenting on the phenomenon of *stereotype threat* (the disruptive threat of stereotype-driven judgments and treatments) that many identities (e.g., being Black, White, Latinx, LGBTQ+, or diagnosed with depression, cancer, or other conditions) have to contend with in our schools—these threats that play a role in some of society's most difficult challenges. A question I often get about this work is, "What can be done about it?"

In that respect, I have been deeply gratified by the work of a team of educators and educational researchers—Dorothy Steele, Becki Cohn-Vargas, Alexandrea Creer Kahn, Kathe Gogolewski, and Amy Epstein. They have developed research-based systems of application based on ideas that I think, it is now fair to say, are beginning to take root in American classrooms. Three previous books on identity safety have given teachers and administrators concrete blueprints for how to foster belongingness in diverse classrooms, and that, in so doing, have helped mightily in reducing group achievement gaps that so plague our society. These are remarkable books, books that answer that basic question about what to do with feasible, humane, and effective strategies and practices. Things that work.

But until now, there has been little written on building essential partnerships with families. *Identity Safe Spaces at Home and School: Partnering to Overcome Inequity,* cowritten by Becki Cohn-Vargas and Debbie Zacarian, both renowned authors and scholars, remedies that situation. It is a groundbreaking book that brings the Identity Safety framework to bear on all we do. It is both practical and insightful. But it especially brings into view the tremendous power that parent-school partnerships can have in overcoming inequity. There is no better time for this book to arrive. In the wake of the pandemic and the challenges it has brought to families and schools, I, for one, am deeply gratified to see it. It is an important note of hope in these truly challenging times.

—*Claude Steele*

Acknowledgments

Twenty-nine people courageously share their personal life experiences; their portraits span ages from 10 to 70 years old; roles as children, youth, parents, and educators; locations throughout the United States; and represent diverse racial, cultural, linguistic, ethnic, and gender identities, sexual orientations, and neurodiversities. Their stories bring the principles of our book to life and speak to the heart of what identity safety means in our ever-changing world. We are grateful to Carlee Adamson, Judy Appel, Tris Appel-Bernstein, Alison Bernstein, Daniel Chan, Susan Charles, Catherine Clune and her daughter, Lulu, Lori Davis, Michelle Gahee, Lenore Harris, Sameer Jha, Jesús Mena, Alexandrea Creer Kahn, Kenny Kahn, Melania Khouie-Vargas, Chen Kong-Wick, Rebecca Mikulski, Vincent Pompei, Paula Rabideaux, Lorianna Seidlitz-Smith, Oswaldo Torres, Pooja Tilvawala, Randi Thomson-Story, Isacc Villanueva, Sonia Patel, Louise Bay Waters, and Lisha Wilson.

We also acknowledge many scholars whose research informed our understanding of identity safety. The oft-used metaphor *We stand on the shoulders of giants* applies to three leading scholars and contributors to this work. These include Claude Steele, the imminent social psychologist whose seminal work on stereotype threat led to the theory of identity safety; Dorothy Steele, the educational researcher whose contributions in this field, particularly on teacher behaviors that lead to a student's sense of identity safety and academic achievement, greatly expand its application in classroom settings; and Kenneth Hardy, clinical psychologist and researcher who helps us all see and better understand the phenomenon of racial trauma.

Special thanks go to the many people from Teachers College Press (TCP) who made this book possible. We appreciate James Banks, preeminent multicultural education scholar and TCP author, who introduced us to Brian Ellerbeck, executive acquisitions editor. Brian graciously paired us with Allison Scott, senior acquisitions editor—special thanks to Allison for supporting our efforts to authentically portray the enduring values of identity safety.

No book could ever be written without the support, patience, and love of family. Becki thanks her husband, Rito Vargas, and children, Priscilla

Vargas, Melania Khouie-Vargas, and Luna Vargas, and grandson, Anteo Khouie-Vargas, and the beautiful intersections of their diverse extended family. Becki also acknowledges her parents, who are no longer alive, and sisters, who continue to influence her deep commitment to working for justice and equity and bridging cultural and other differences.

Debbie thanks her husband, Matt, and children, Katie and Jackie, and parents and grandparents, including members of our family who bravely fled their homelands.

The promise of identity safety came alive through the inspiration of all who contributed to this collaborative effort.

Introduction

This book is written as a resource for educators with the most up-to-date research on identity safety as it applies to our ever-changing, ever-growing multidiverse student and family communities. What do we mean by multidiverse? Society is changing rapidly. We are much more racially, culturally, linguistically, and ethnically diverse and, as importantly, much more aware of LGBTQ+ and neurodiverse communities. As such, we use the asset-based term, *multidiverse,* to reflect the rich backgrounds and social identities of all the underrepresented students, educators, families, and others with whom we work and socialize. The intent of our book is on building identity safe practices at school and supporting these to occur at home.

The urgency for our book is as multifold as is our focus on multidiverse student needs in our ever-changing, evolving society. During the past decade, educators have become much more aware of the epic number of children experiencing adverse childhood experiences. Additionally, the COVID-19 pandemic illuminated the disproportionate number of people from underrepresented populations who had a higher risk of contracting and dying from the virus because of inequitable access to food, shelter, and medical care (C-Span, 2020). Further, while we are becoming a more diverse society, the voices of some parents/guardians and local and state-level politicians are calling for restrictions to much-needed culturally responsive, social, and emotional learning [SEL], and identity safe approaches (Anderson, 2022). Also, colorblind practices that ignore the voices of multidiverse families and prohibit teaching about their historic and lived experiences is a barrier to inclusion (Markus et al., 2000). For example, in some states, crucial topics such as the history of racism, discussions of diversity, and many books on these topics have been banned (PEN America, 2022). Another important factor is that transgender students have been targeted by laws that take away their rights (Krishnakumar, 2021). Florida, for example, has enacted laws prohibiting educators from teaching these matters under penalty of being sued or fired (Najarro, 2022).

These trends urgently call for an approach to interrupt the cycle of inequities that have occurred for generations and provide a counter to practices that seek to undermine the capacity for all students to flourish. Instead, practices that cultivate diversity as a resource for learning must be amplified.

Identity safe teaching is a widely known evidence-based approach where student identities are validated and valued in a welcoming environment that counteracts the negative impacts of oppression. Its foundation was derived from research done by seminal scholars Steele and Aronson (1995) on the effect of stereotype threat on intellectual performance. While Steele and Aronson's research focused on college-age students, the Stanford Integrated Schools Project (SISP) large-scale research study focused on grade-school students (Steele & Cohn-Vargas, 2013) and drew from the findings of Steele and Aronson. Namely, when educators validate a child's social identities and support them with child-centered practices in a caring environment, they feel identity safe and do better in school. This book applies the research further to include the positive possibilities that can happen when these practices are applied by educators and families to support children to flourish in school and in their lives. In addition to the research on identity safety, it also applies the preponderance of research that demonstrates the effectiveness of a strengths-based and culturally responsive approach.

Our professional contributions led us to this coauthored project. Each of us brings years of scholarship on the benefits of working in partnership with families. When children hear a synchronized message of identity safety at home and in school, it has the potential to exponentially expand the positive effects of identity safety. Our hope is that this book breaks new ground on the power of home-school partnerships to overcome inequities.

Our book reflects a core belief that all professionals who work on behalf of children have an essential role in enacting and sustaining copartnerships with families. This stance reflects changing trends in education where students' academic and social–emotional outcomes are greatly enhanced when we copartner with families to support identity safe practices. Such practices can enhance a child's development—physical, psychological, cognitive, social, and emotional—while reducing biological impediments to learning, such as stress and anxiety (Darling-Hammond & Cook-Harvey, 2018). We believe that a deeper understanding of the nuances of our many identities will aid us in understanding how to nurture and safeguard diverse identities at home and in school.

*   *   *

A unique aspect of this book is the generous contributions from educators, parents/guardians, adults, and youth we interviewed. Each chapter includes theoretical foundations of the concepts explored and contributors' voices (what we call Shining a Light) to highlight a key idea. Each chapter also has Reflection spaces for readers to consider how to enact the fundamental principles, concepts, and strategies presented. We also counter misinformation and provide statistics, and examples of how we can support all children's identities. While we encourage the participation of parents/guardians, we want to ensure that the voices of some critics do not undermine the identity safety of multidiverse students and families. Each chapter also includes big ideas, enduring values, and specific home and school approaches to support identity safety.

Chapter 1, Understanding Identity Safety, introduces the concept and research on identity safety and why it matters. It examines attitudes and behaviors that undermine identity safety, including othering, stereotype threat, and colorblind practices where differences are ignored. It highlights the urgency for fostering pride and embracing diversity. Additionally, it introduces a schema for home-school partnerships that includes a Working Group to guide our efforts.

Chapter 2, Creating a Culture of Caring, presents a starting point for identity safe home-school partnerships by forming a culture of caring and compassion and building partnerships with multidiverse students and families. It highlights the urgency for the moving from a deficit- to an asset-based approach and the importance of listening in all we do to support home-school interactions.

Chapter 3, Understanding Our Own Identity, focuses on how educators can support identity safety by reflecting on our identities, values, and beliefs and considering the multidiverse experiences and cultural values that are very different from our own, the prevalence of students with adverse childhood experiences, and the urgency for examining implicit and explicit biases. We highlight mutually respectful and nonhierarchical home-school partnerships and offer practices for facilitating multidiverse teams to foster belonging and participation.

Chapter 4, Supporting Positive Identity Development, explores research on supporting racial, cultural, linguistic, ethnic, and gender identity development, and the intersections of multiple identities. We also explore ways for fostering students' identity as competent learners. We highlight the importance of learning from and with parents/guardians and offer tools for engaging in conversations about multidiverse identities. We also discuss the importance of accurate portrayals of history from many perspectives.

Chapter 5, Harnessing the Power of Connectedness, Cooperation, and Compassion, examines fostering positive interpersonal relationships, promoting cooperation and compassion, self-awareness, managing emotions, empathy, and relational skills. It explores ways to embrace multidiversity, cooperation, and interdependence. It includes ways for partnering with parents/guardians.

Chapter 6, Building Empowerment, Agency, and Resilience, explores the foundational principles that support empowering children as autonomous learners who are resilient and have agency in their lives. It discusses the importance of student empowerment through developing the skills of receptiveness and assertiveness and a positive academic identity and provides a schema of the different stages of empowerment development and offers strategies for supporting these to occur at home and school. We share home-school partnerships to foster student and parent/guardian identity safety and empowerment.

Chapter 7, Moving Away From "Same Old Habits" to Professional Growth, discusses the changing role that educators can enact to support identity safe practices at home. It includes a cycle of identity safety inquiry and provides professional growth tools for evaluating, strengthening, and celebrating home-school partnerships.

HOW TO READ THIS BOOK

Our book is intended for pre-K–12 educators (including teachers, school principals, specialists, counselors, and other stakeholders) who are looking to create identity safe schools, classrooms, and, as important, home-school partnerships. We encourage the use of this book in educational courses in institutions of higher education and professional growth experiences in schools, districts, organizations, and agencies (including educational service agencies that provide professional development experiences).

The chapters are intended to be read in succession and build on one another. Our hope is that readers will work through the materials found in this book, obtain a collective language and understanding of identity safety as it applies to equity, diversity and inclusion, and engage in dialogue, reflection tasks, and actions to cultivate and to enact the concepts. Developing a shared language and practice is essential for building identity safe home-school partnerships in which children flourish.

We believe that every educator and educator-in-training, educational specialist and specialist-in-training, and leader and leader-in-training can and do impact students in a powerful way. Our book is intended to honor and affirm the strengths that educators, families, and students possess so that we may collectively take actions to foster and cultivate identity safe practices and ways of being and acting that support students to succeed in school and in their lives. In this spirit, we begin our first chapter by exploring the concept of and research on identity safety and why it matters.

CHAPTER 1

Understanding Identity Safety

In 3rd grade, some 6th graders cornered me in the restroom and began doing what often happened to me, homophobic bullying, using really awful pejoratives, and pushing me. Then, they grabbed me, held me upside down over the toilet, and dunked my head in. They continued to flush the toilet over and over and over again as if they were trying to flush me down the toilet to get rid of me. I thought to myself, "I'm going to drown." And then they laughed and finally left me soaking wet and crying. So, I kind of composed myself and returned to class, and the teacher asked me, "Why are you all wet? Why are you playing in the water?" I didn't respond. I had to stand outside the classroom and was not allowed to go to recess because I was "playing in the water and got myself all wet." Of course, I didn't tell her what happened because I was worried that my teacher would then suspect I might be what those students called me. I was terrified that she would call home and tell my family. I worried about how my family might react. I feared I had let them down and worried how they would treat me if they found out I was this identity that society, my peers, and many individuals in my family thought was so awful. Due to the pervasive homophobia and gender-based bias I was exposed to, I had an internal battle again and again. I felt like I had a good heart, but I had this really negative stain, you know, it was really difficult to grapple with those emotions again at such a young age. I didn't accept my identity until I was in college and eventually began to come out to close friends and family. Today, I feel proud of my LGBTQ+ identity, although it hurts to see how many in society still have negative biases about LGBTQ+ people.

> Vincent (Vinnie) Pompei is a professor in the doctoral program
> for educational leadership at San Diego State University

Many children, like Vinnie, are bullied, teased, or excluded because of the way they look, the way they speak, and the qualities that might make them different from their peers. Some are stigmatized because they belong to multidiverse groups.

Members of these multidiverse groups are subject to bullying, bias, and hate because of their actual or perceived race, ethnicity, language difference, religion, gender identity, sexual orientation, and physical, mental, and learning disabilities. Also, many children harbor feelings of shame in isolation. For example, Vinnie never shared his feelings of shame with anyone until he was 19 years old, when he started accepting his gay identity.

In our introduction, we highlighted the importance of identity safe environments where each child's identity is valued and treated as an asset and where all are welcomed as contributive members of their community. This is true for children of all backgrounds, especially those from histori-cally marginalized groups.

As stated in the introduction, this book is a groundbreaking effort to illustrate the power of home-school partnerships to foster identity safety. The urgency for creating identity safe spaces for students is particularly poignant in the current divisive climate where new laws, policies, and the loud voices of some parents who oppose diversity and equity have under-mined positive identity development for multidiverse students. A home-school partnership for identity safety offers the promise of inclusion and validation for students of all backgrounds.

In this chapter, we deepen the understanding of identity safety and in-troduce how to foster it at home and in school, including an exploration of

- what identity safety is, and why it matters;
- the impact of othering, stereotype threat, and colorblindness where differences are ignored;
- identity safe teaching as evidenced-based research;
- the urgency for taking action; and
- introducing identity safety through forming a Working Group to foster partnership between home and school.

For children and youth, identity safety flows from a person's sense that their identity is an asset. As they gain self-confidence, they also learn to embrace differences and develop compassion for others. In this chapter, we set three important goals for educators and families to create and sustain identify safe spaces:

1. Give children rich, positive experiences that continuously affirm their multiple and varied identities.
2. Support awareness and offer tools to deconstruct, dismantle, and counteract the power of the negative stereotypes about identity.

3. Help children come to celebrate different social identities and to cultivate diversity as a rich shared resource.

WHAT IS IDENTITY SAFETY, AND WHY DOES IT MATTER?

As children grow up, they ask, "Who am I?" and "How do I fit into the world around me?" Across history, philosophers, psychologists, and religious scholars have debated and wrestled with these questions. Social psychologists describe the continual interplay of individual and group identity.

> Identity cannot be achieved or maintained by oneself alone. Identity is formed in a social context. It is a social process that is interdependent with one's ongoing interactions. Through engagement with and recognition by others, an individual becomes a person, and identities are conferred. (Markus et al., 2000 p. 236)

Paula Moya and Michael Hames-Garcia (2000) use the metaphor of colors in a photograph to describe how social identities intersect within each of us (e.g., female, first-generation Latinx, sister, brother, teacher.) At times, race, ethnicity, sexuality, gender, and social class, to name a few, are visible in distinct colors, while at other times, they blend and swirl. Moreover, our identities are situated in social and historical contexts, influenced by power, privilege, and status. Over time, we are impacted by affirming, joyful, and motivating experiences and by alienating, frightening, and traumatic ones.

A child's first significant influences come from the parents and guardians who raise them. They also come from immediate family members who live in the same household (such as grandparents, siblings, and other caregivers). As children continue to develop, they absorb additional impressions from peers, teachers, and the community. From infancy, the larger world communicates subtle and not-so-subtle attitudes about identity, sometimes crystal clear but often confusing and contradictory. Every child needs support to navigate the myriad of messages they receive. A sense of identity safety should be a safe harbor where a child feels (1) firmly anchored and confident about who they are and (2) prepared to thrive in a diverse, global world. We communicate a sense of identity safety by fostering the positive aspects of their identity. We help young people build resilience to counteract negative messages, harmful treatment, and exclusion that can leave lifelong scars. It requires that we illuminate and address three significant obstacles: othering, stereotype threat, and colorblind practices that undermine a person's sense of identity safety.

The Impact of Othering

john powell (n.d.) (lowercase intentional) describes "the problem of the 21st century as the problem of "othering."

> Othering is defined as "processes of exclusion, marginalization, and structural inequality" . . . [Belonging includes] "having a meaningful voice and the opportunity to participate in the design of political, social, and cultural structures that shape one's life—the right to both contribute and make demands upon society and political institutions. At its core, structural belonging holds a radically inclusive vision because it requires mutual power, access, and opportunity among all groups and individuals within a shared container (such as a society, organization, club, etc.)." (paras. 1, 3)

Othering plays out at individual and systemic levels through microaggressions, discrimination exclusion, and in acts of violence and hate. Othering has always been expressed through worldwide patterns of oppression, and bias exacerbated for multidiverse people, including people of color, religious minorities, members of the LGBTQ+ community, individuals with disabilities, undocumented immigrants, and others. Recently, members of these groups have experienced an uptick in hate crimes with the mainstreaming of white nationalism and white supremacist ideologies (Stern, 2022). In addition, these ideologies have included antidemocratic and authoritarian beliefs spurred on by fear and fueled by misinformation, conspiracy theories, and fake news. They have also been enacted through voter suppression, legislation targeting gay and transgender individuals, discrimination in schools, book censorship, and laws outlawing the teaching of accurate accounts of history (Green, 2023; Okeowo, 2016).

Othering has also been experienced by many of the contributors to this book. They share personal stories of othering that never reached the ears of their parents/guardians or educators.

Shining a Light on Othering

Two examples show how devastating othering can be. The first is from Kenny Kahn, a school principal and father of two young sons. He wrote an article (Kahn 2020) about an experience that happened during the pandemic:

I have been wearing a mask out in public . . . I follow the health and social distancing guidelines in public areas out of respect. But I'm a big, Black guy, and Black and Brown men who cover their faces are perceived as a threat, as unpredictable, as dangerous. In the last two weeks, at local parks and hiking areas, I have been described as looking like a murderer. One woman out walking her dog ran away from me for dear life. . . . . All of this while [I was] in the company of my two-year-old son, Theo. I don't know what to tell him. . . .

I've had cashiers not accept checks after customers ahead of me have had theirs accepted without question. . . . I've been asked to leave the premises immediately for reasons I can only imagine. I often bite my tongue, choose my words and actions wisely . . . My motto is to lead with love and compassion in my personal and professional life. But just because I am a jolly good fellow, it doesn't mean that I don't have things that pull at me and affect me to my core. (2020, paras. 2–3)

Our second example is Lisha, a physician whose daughter just started college. Lisha tells us that her childhood experience as the only Black student in her elementary school was generally positive. She had many friends and, in rare instances when someone called her a racial slur, her White classmates stood up for her. However, as the only Black girl in middle school, she had a deeply wounding experience of othering.

In physical education, we learned square dancing. Our gym teacher would line up the boys on one side of the gym and the girls on the other. Then she'd tell the boys to pick a partner. So, the boys would head out to pick their partners. And every single darn time, I would be left standing there with Sally. I was the only Black kid in the class, and Sally was White and overweight. I'm telling you that wrecked me; it had such a profound effect. I am still scarred to this day. I don't understand why humans do this; you would think that the teacher, a grown woman, would have noticed and stepped in and done something. That she would have had a couple of the 4 or 5 extra boys, take Sally and me as a partner. But she did nothing. It was really tough, feeling the shame, feeling naked, really naked, standing there.

Like Vinnie, Lisha hid her shame and told no one about it. Unfortunately, similar incidents occur daily. As educators and parents/guardians, we must become more aware and better equipped to respond to what is happening to children and take action to support them. This is especially true in the current climate, where there has been an uptick in acts of othering, bias, and hate toward marginalized groups (Levin et al., 2022).

 Reflection Task

1. How might an experience of othering like Kenny's or Lisha's cause deep wounds that impact a person over a long time?

2. Describe an experience of othering that either you or someone you know has experienced.
3. How can the current divisive political environment increase a sense of being othered to a multidiverse person's experience even if it does not happen directly to them?

What Is Stereotype Threat?

Stereotype threat is a phenomenon that can harm or limit life opportunities when an individual or group of individuals face or perceive the possibility of facing a negative stereotype in a particular circumstance (Steele, 1997). Even when a person believes that negative stereotypes about their group are inaccurate, the fear of inadvertently confirming the stereotypes can harm them and limit their life prospects (Steele, 1997). A seminal investigation into the dynamics of stereotype threat was undertaken by Steele and Aronson in 1995. Their investigation involved a dual study of two groups of Black and White students, all possessing comparable aptitudes.

Participants from both study groups were tasked with a segment of the Graduate Record Exam. The first group was told that the examination would evaluate their intellectual prowess, while the second was informed that the test held no bearing on their intellect. The results of the two study groups revealed some noteworthy insights. Specifically, the Black students performed less successfully than their White counterparts in the first group and Black and White students in the second group. This discrepancy is attributed, in part, to the phenomenon of stereotype threat that the first group of Black students experienced concerning the assessment of intelligence. An additional finding is of note. Specifically, Black students in the second group achieved the same high scores as their White peers across both groups. This underscores the role of stereotype threat in influencing performance disparities.

Following the initial research, thousands of stereotype threat studies have been repeated with people of all ages negatively stereotyped by race, gender, and other multidiverse identities. The results consistently show a person's performance is reduced under stereotype threat conditions (Spencer et al., 2016). Claude Steele (1999) explained that it is possible to "create niches in which negative stereotypes are not felt to apply," and thereby the negative stereotypes will not limit the impact on academic success for African American students (sec. 5, para. 13). Steele (2011) concluded, "if enough cues in a setting can lead members of a group to feel "identity safe" it might neutralize the impact of other cues that could otherwise threaten them"

(p. 147). Schools can work to counteract the impact of stereotype threat by building trust with students and families through identity safe practices that respect their ways of being and living. This can occur when students feel confident to express their authentic identities in a space where differences are not ignored.

Colorblindness as a Barrier to Inclusion

Some teachers have been heard saying, "I don't care if a student is red, green, black, blue, or what-have-you. I treat everyone the same." With this "colorblind" stance, they claim not to notice racial differences. However, this is impossible in a world highly stratified by race and ethnicity (Markus et al., 2000). Nevertheless, studies have found that starting with preschool, most educators employ a colorblind approach (Husband, 2012).

Attempts to erase cultural differences in a vast "melting pot" are not new. Paula Rabideaux, an educator and member of the Menominee tribe, explains, "Both my parents, my four grandparents, and all eight of my great-grandparents attended boarding school. Government schools prevented them from learning our history, language, and culture" (Cohn-Vargas & Rabideaux, 2023). These schools gave Native American children Anglo-American names, forced them to wear Western clothing, and abandon their way of life. In these schools, children were told they were inferior (Little, 2018). Such schools did not stop the brutal mistreatment of Native Americans, including those who attempted to assimilate.

Additional reasons point to why colorblind practices are problematic. When differences are ignored, people can feel invisible and silenced. Children pick up on subtle cues that come from not seeing themselves represented. They may feel their acceptance is conditional and must withhold parts of themselves and assimilate to fit in. Efforts to ignore differences can lead to othering for students, even at young ages.

Shining a Light on Colorblind Teaching

Nicole observed the following conversation between several children during her student-teaching assignment.

> I was student teaching in a 1st-grade class when two students, a boy and a girl, sitting at the same table, discovered that they both spoke Tagalog. They got excited and started saying different words to each other. Then, suddenly, another student at the table jumped in and said, "I can speak gibberish." and proceeded to babble away, making a bunch of different noises.

So, one of the Tagalog speakers replied, "You don't even know what we're saying." Then the teacher came over to the children who spoke Tagalog, saying, "We've been learning a lot about being inclusive and making sure everyone feels included. So, it's really important that no one feels left out. So, you should speak English with people at school."

 Reflection Task

Reflect on Nicole's story.

1. What actions did the teacher take that you believe were not helpful?
2. What actions would you have taken to demonstrate an intent to be inclusive toward all students?

Although this teacher might have perceived that she was fostering inclusion, she was essentially silencing the two Tagalog speakers who had found a unique opportunity to connect around their shared language. The third child, while trying to fit in, was also unintentionally undermining their language. The teacher might have used this teachable moment to validate the Tagalog-speaking children's language. She might have invited the Tagalog speakers to teach the other child a few words in Tagalog. She also might have clarified that gibberish is not a language while taking care not to make that child feel bad. This was a tiny moment in a long schooling process, but it was a teachable moment that essentially opted for color-blindness rather than validating the students' language. For many multilingual learners, being limited from speaking their own language is a form of cultural erasure that can lead to rejection of their home language.

Our desire to avoid discomfort can impede how we support identity safe spaces for all our students and others. We can erroneously assume that discrimination and racism will disappear by avoiding interactions about them. Researcher Jessica Sullivan (2020) explains that studies in the United States found that by 9 months old, babies can categorize faces by race. By 3 years old, some children have negative associations with some racial groups resulting in attitudes leading to racial discrimination by the time children enter school.

Patterns of cultural erasure and "colorblind practices" also can be life-threatening. For example, recent legislation, sometimes described as "don't say gay" laws, seek to erase the identities of LGBTQ+ students. Thirty-three U.S. states have introduced more than 100 bills that curb the rights of transgender people. For example, an Arkansas bill says educators must refer to children only by their "biological sex" indicated on their birth certificates. An Iowa bill requires parental consent for educators to discuss gender identity in the classroom. In other states, medical gender interventions and hormone blockers have been outlawed for children despite being approved by the American Academy of Pediatrics (Krishnakumar, 2021).

The devaluation of trans identities resulting from these laws can have devastating and life-threatening results. A national survey of a diverse sample of 34,000 LGBTQ+ youth ages 13–24 by the Trevor Project in 2022 revealed that an epic number, 45%, of LGBTQ+ youth have considered suicide. Additionally, LGBTQ+ students who felt a high degree of social support from their families reported attempting suicide at less than half the rate of those who did not feel supported (The Trevor Project, 2022).

Family rejection has been found to be the most significant cause of suicidal tendencies, self-harm, and completed suicides by LGBTQ+ students (Ryan et al., 2010). Schools with affirming practices of LGBTQ+ identities reported lower rates of suicide attempts (The Trevor Project, 2022). We will offer specific suggestions for home-school partnerships to support identity safety for LGBTQ+ students in Chapter 5.

Identity Safe Teaching as an Antidote to Stereotype Threat, Othering, and Colorblind Teaching

Claude and Dorothy Steele coined the term "identity safe teaching" in the 1990s to counteract the impact of stereotype threat. The Steeles (Steele, C. M., 2011) hypothesized that if schools started validating each student's identity early, they could shield children from some negative impacts of society's stereotypes and prejudices. They also recognized that this validation would need to come from multiple sources. Children would need to feel validated by seeing people like them represented on the classroom walls and in the curriculum and by feedback given to them about their potential. The validation would need to be consistent with schoolwide discipline practices and in every interaction between adults and students and among students.

The Steeles embarked on a research study known as the Stanford Integrated Schools Project (SISP) (Steele, C. M., 2011; Steele, D. M., 2012). The study aimed to identify teacher behaviors that lead to student identity safety. It involved observing 1,753 1st-, 3rd-, and 5th-grade students in 84 classrooms in an urban California school district. The results showed that when teachers used a set of specific teaching practices, students from all ethnic groups (African American, Latinx, Asian, and White) felt more identity safe, liked school more, and performed higher on standardized assessments.

The researchers categorized the practices found in higher identity safe classes into 4 primary domains and 12 components (see Figure 1.1) (Cohn-Vargas, 2007; Cohn-Vargas & Steele, 2016; Steele, D. M. & Cohn-Vargas, 2013).

The SISP study led to coauthor Becki's subsequent research to richly describe the components and translate them into actionable teaching strategies in K–12 classrooms (Cohn-Vargas, 2007). It also led to three coauthored books on identity safe classroom and school practices (Cohn-Vargas et al., 2021, 2022; Steele, D. M. & Cohn-Vargas, 2013).

Bolstering Identity Safety With a Strengths-Based Stance

The findings from the SISP study are reinforced by the preponderance of research that points to the importance of acknowledging and valuing each student's unique personal, social, cultural, language, and academic attributes. Abraham Maslow (1999) first introduced the urgency of focusing our attention and actions on the positive attributes that all humans possess instead of focusing on deficits. Expert education scholars Moll et al. (2005) demonstrated the importance of using such an approach with families. They coined the term "funds of knowledge" to describe the expertise and skills that all families possess and pass on to their children and the importance of educators acknowledging and integrating these into our work

Figure 1.1. Domains and Components of Identity Safe Teaching

1. Student-Centered Teaching
     Listening for Student Voices
     Teaching for Understanding
     Focus on Cooperation
     Classroom Autonomy

2. Cultivating Diversity as a Resource
     Using Diversity as a Resource for Teaching
     High Expectations and Academic Rigor
     Challenging Curriculum

3. Classroom Relationships
     Teacher Warmth and Availability to Support Learning
     Positive Student Relationships

4. Caring Classrooms Environments
     Teacher Skill
     Emotional and Physical Comfort
     Attention to Prosocial Development

with students. This research is also bolstered by psychologist Carol Dweck's (2006) research. She examined the importance of believing in students' endless capacities to learn and achieve and supporting them to do the same. Her research findings support using a strengths-based approach, particularly with children who have experienced adversity and are reared in communities with few resources (Dweck et al., 2014).

It is not that these researchers ignored the adversities that so many children experienced or that they advocate that we ignore these. Their findings point to the importance that we must pay as much, if not more, attention to the strengths and capacities that such children possess inherently or as a result of facing adversity (Zacarian et al., 2017). Indeed, overcoming inequities is possible by identifying and drawing from students' and families' strengths and partnering with them on this endeavor (Zacarian & Soto, 2020; Zacarian & Silverstone, 2020). The preponderance of research on strengths-based practices is also bolstered by what we know as culturally sustaining practices.

Advancing Identity Safety Through Culturally Sustaining Practices

One of the most influential contributors to what we know about learning is Lev Vygotsky (1978). A developmental psychologist, he posited that learning involves (1) interactions in a familiar sociocultural context and (2) thinking as a learner. An example of what this means is the following word problem:

> Abby will take a 7-hour trip on the Acela train from Boston, MA, to Washington, DC. James will make an 8-hour trip on the Northeast Regional train from Boston to Washington, DC. How much faster is Abby's train than James'? Why is it faster?

The first part of the question involves having familiarity with the difference between the ACELA and Northeast Regional trains. The former stops less often, includes first- and business-class seats, and covers less distance than the latter. The second part of the question requires that we use our mathematical thinking skills to apply the formula distance = rate ÷ time. However, without knowing the crucial sociocultural differences between the two trains, we might assume that they cover the exact same route and that one, therefore, is traveling much faster than the other. While our example is between two American cities, we can easily see how this example might be even more challenging if it were in a language we do not understand and a context we are unfamiliar with.

For students to be able to learn, they must have cultural knowledge of the subject matter being studied; the ability to listen, speak, read, and write in that language; prior academic experiences in the area of study so that they can make meaning of what is being learned; and the ability to think as learners (Zacarian, 2013. The foundations of culturally sustaining pedagogy reflected these attributes (Zacarian & Soto, 2020). Gloria Ladson-Billings, a seminal scholar in culturally sustaining practices, defines it as a pedagogy in which students are "empowered intellectually, socially, emotionally, and politically (because it uses) cultural referents to impart knowledge, skills, and attitudes" (Ladson-Billings, 1994, p. 20). Further, Ladson-Billings (1995) outlines three elements of culturally responsive teaching that bolsters the research on identity safety: (1) having high expectations for each student's capacity to learn, (2) using culturally relevant teaching to support positive cultural identity; and (3) supporting students to be empowered to take a critical stance against and interrupt inequities.

In this book, we have added home-school partnerships to increase the power and sustain the influence of identity safety by using a strengths-based, culturally responsive approach. We draw from an abundance of research on the critical importance of family–school engagement (Epstein et al., 2019; Moll et al., 2005; Robles de Meléndez & Beck, 2019), our scholarship and insights gathered from our interviews share practices that promote a continuous set of experiences that foster and sustain identity safety, enhanced through partnerships between home and school.

TAKING ACTION

There is great urgency for parents/guardians and educators to become aware and understand the nuances of diverse social identities. We need to create conditions for children to develop positive identities and find ways to counteract the effect of othering, stereotype threat, and colorblind practices.

An Alternative to Colorblind Teaching

Kris Gutiérrez and Barbara Rogoff (2003) offer an alternative to ignoring differences that seeks to avoid stereotyping groups. They coined the term "repertoires of practice," referring to practices rather than traits to encompass some commonalities shared by different cultures or identities while acknowledging wide variation among people with similar backgrounds. They explain that referring to a specific "trait" assumes that a particular characteristic applies to every group member, running the risk of stereotyping that group. Making generalized statements about a group's traits assumes every group member has these fixed characteristics. Students can share from their repertoires of practice and lived experiences (Gutiérrez & Correa-Chavez, 2006; Gutiérrez & Rogoff, 2003).

Shining a Light on Identity Influences

Here we offer two examples of how parents/guardians can intentionally consider ways to help their children navigate the complexity of identity influences. In our first example, we meet Lulu, whose White adoptive parents offer opportunities for her to befriend Ethiopians. She attends a science program with many Ethiopian immigrant students. Lulu explains:

> I'm a 7th grader. I was adopted as a baby from Ethiopia, that's important for my identity. I'm Black, and that's important for my identity.

> There are a lot of Ethiopians there. We have potlucks where I get to try a lot of Ethiopian food. In addition to being born there and living for 9 months, my parents took me to visit Ethiopia.

However, at school, Lulu encountered classmates who questioned her identity based on erroneous stereotypes.

> They either think I'm mixed or don't think I'm African American at all; even though I was born in Africa, I'm completely African. Because of stereotypes, people assume that Africans are supposed to have wider features and dark skin, while I have lighter skin and my features are skinnier because I'm from East Africa and not West Africa. I probably have Saudi Arabian or Yemenite heritage too. But at the end of the day, I am African. Stereotypes like that damage your identity when you have somebody saying, "No, you can't be who you are because you don't align with what I think you should look like."

> In the second example, we meet Susan, born on the Caribbean Island of Dominica; she and her husband, Jeff, raised her four daughters in the United States, where she worked as a school counselor and principal and now runs an educational leadership master's degree program. Susan explains:

> > Our family is multiracial. In the Caribbean, we don't talk a whole lot about race. Whether you're White or Black, race is not something we spend a lot of time concerned about. I'm incredibly fortunate that being a Black person in the Caribbean is viewed as an asset.

> > However, coming to the United States, we knew we were coming into a racist society and would be experiencing something different than we had ever experienced before. So, we banded together with other members of the Caribbean

immigrant community to protect our children. We all decided our job was to protect our children from the enemy: hate and racism. We would do everything in our power to ensure our children would not feel less than others. We were not going to let this happen. It was very, very deliberate.

We made sure that our kids learned about West Indian culture. In addition to our trips home, we make sure that they have books about who we are and where we came from. Every holiday our community gets together as a family, and all the children call all of us Uncle and Auntie.

 Reflection Task

Reflect on the ways families and schools can work to reinforce positive identity development.

1. Describe 2–3 ways that Lulu's parents and Susan and her husband supported their children to feel safe, a sense of belonging, value, and competence.
2. How did Lulu's experience of having others define her identity cause her to feel othered and that their actions harmed her identity development?
3. How can schools reinforce positive identity development in concert with families?

Fostering Pride

Lulu's parents and Susan and her husband intentionally took action to foster pride in their children's identities. We can help children foster a deep sense of pride in their background by communicating love for their cultures and backgrounds in many forms with thoughtful words and sharing traditions. Fostering pride can happen in ways that are at once simple but also frequently repeated. Oswaldo is 10 years old. His Salvadoran parents met in the United States, and their two children were born in Texas.

Honestly, my dad says El Salvador is one of the best countries in the world. My mother tells me that El Salvador looks absolutely wonderful. All the time, she tells me, "One day you'll go there, and you will love the beaches and everything else."

Pooja is 27 years old and a leader in the international youth climate movement. She was born in Gujarat, India, and came to the United States as an infant. She just returned from a visit with her relatives.

India offers a heightened sensory experience, and I miss it when I return home from a visit. I love the smell of spices, the colorful clothing, and the refreshing taste of coconut water. I am proud of our deep and ancient history, including the world's oldest religion—Hinduism. I love celebrating our rich cultures; it's as if each state is its own country with local languages, cuisines, clothing, and traditions. We have endured and built much resilience to colonization to maintain our cultural and historical richness and depth.

Pride in one's background may not be in question for people who have grown up without experiencing aspects of their identity being marginalized, stigmatized, or oppressed. However, for those whose groups have been stigmatized, pride and dignity are paramount to counteract the many judgments and stereotypes, whether overtly or implicitly expressed. In the Merriam-Webster Dictionary (n.d.), one definition of pride is "respect and appreciation for oneself and others as members of a group, especially a marginalized group: solidarity with a group based on a shared identity, history, and experience."

Whole movements have grown around feeling pride after one's people have been harmed and made to feel shame. For example, my (Becki's) parents had their German citizenship stripped because they were Jewish and had to flee the Nazis. While they survived, my father's grandmother and other relatives were murdered in concentration camps. I never articulated it as a child, but I remember wondering, "Why do they hate us? What is wrong with us?" Then, in 10th grade, our Hebrew School teacher, Mr. Vogel, taught us to be proud to be Jews. That echoed many of my parents' messages expressing value in our Jewish heritage.

Pride is cultivated in many ways, by sharing music, traditions, and histories. In 1968, in the documentary *Mr. Dynamite: The Rise of James Brown*, (Irwin, 2020) Al Sharpton recounts Brown telling him,

> "I said to myself, 'we've lost our pride.'" That night, Brown went to his hotel room and wrote the lyrics to "Say It Loud (I'm Black and I'm Proud)" on a napkin. In the spur of the moment, it became a song that literally changed the social dynamics of the United States.

Here is the refrain:

> Say it loud; I'm Black, I'm Proud.
> We're people. We like the birds and the bees,
> We'd rather die on our feet than be living on our knees.
> Say it loud, I'm Black, and I'm proud!
> Say it loud, I'm Black, and I'm proud! (Brown, 1969)

A few years ago, I (Becki) was invited to give a bullying prevention presentation at a meeting of Gay Pride organizers; their goal was to add a component of youth education as part of Pride celebrations. Here I recount the impact of that experience:

> Until that moment, I always viewed Gay Pride marches as demonstrations of resistance and joyful celebrations. I suddenly understood that they are much more. Gay Pride events, now referred to as "Pride," contributed significantly to changing attitudes about LGBTQ+ people.

The first Gay Pride March was created to commemorate the uprising when police raided the Stonewall Inn, a New York City gay bar, in 1969, sparking days of protest and rioting. Now, decades later, yearly Pride events occur around the globe in Amsterdam, Chicago, London, Mexico City, New York, Paris, San Francisco, and São Paulo, and even places where people gather despite resistance. For example, in Iran, where Pride marches are illegal, people risk their lives to participate (HRC Staff, 2019).

Pride flourishes when children see themselves and people like them reflected positively in stories, curricula, movies, and images surrounding them. They feel trust with school staff when they can express themselves in a space free of microaggressions or bullying.

Embracing Diversity

Like pride in one's identity, embracing diversity is also cultivated from infancy and repeated in words and through experiences over many years. For example, when I (Becki) was very young, my mother read us a book entitled *The Churkendoose* (Berenberg, 1946). It was about an animal that was a mixture of a chicken, turkey, goose, and duck. At first, the Churkendoose was rejected by the barnyard animals for being different. Then a fox attacked, and the Churkendoose saved everyone. Ultimately, the Churkendoose declares, "No, no, wait. Before, you caused me tears. Now you're giving me three cheers 'Cause I chased the fox and set you free. Well, I don't want the tears; I don't want the cheers. Can't you like me just because I'm me?" (O'Dell, 2008 para. 14). The story and its message stuck with me my entire life. *The Churkendoose* promotes three key messages: value all identities, create acceptance, and stop bullying and exclusion.

At school, norms of behavior that ensure respect for differences can be woven into all interactions instead of being treated as an add-on. Lesson design can incorporate strategies that deconstruct typical academic hierarchies with activities that equalize the status of all groups in the classroom (Cohn-Vargas et al., 2021).

Noticing Children

At the start of this chapter, we introduced Vinnie and Lisha. Each experienced bullying and exclusion without disclosing their pain to anyone for years. One might ask, "How can we support a child if we do not know they have been mistreated?" Our response is that caring adults, including teachers and parents/guardians, need to develop the skill of *noticing*. We can pay close attention to what a child says *and* what they communicate without words.

Children are constantly changing, yet we can notice patterns and sudden behavioral changes that may signal they feel othered or excluded.

> *Notice their facial expressions:*
> Do they express openness and curiosity, or are they frightened, anxious, and guarded?

> *Notice their interactions:*
> Are their interactions with siblings and peers friendly?
> Do they engage with adults and seek help?
> Do they play with others, or are they often alone?

> *Notice their body language:*
> Are they tense or relaxed?
> Do they smile a lot, or do they frequently furrow their brow?

We can cultivate noticing and listening to support children's expression of their authentic selves while taking action to build confidence and pride in their identities and an openness to people with different identities.

PARTNERSHIPS BETWEEN HOME AND SCHOOL

Home and school environments are the places where children in grades spanning from pre-K–12 can develop positive identities and feel a sense of belonging and agency in loving homes and caring schools by:

- experiencing positive relationships amongst and between the people at home and school;
- understanding different aspects of their evolving identities and feeling confident to express their authentic selves;
- developing agency and increasingly becoming critical thinkers; and
- learning to cooperate with others.

As stated in the Introduction, an authentic partnership between parents/guardians and educators offers great potential to extend the benefits of identity safety for children and youth. Educators also need to consider these qualities as they create an identity safe space for parents/guardians and their children.

Forming a Working Group to Support Identity Safe Home-School Partnerships

Identity safety home-school partnerships begin by welcoming multidiverse partners in an atmosphere of trust and inclusion. Child psychiatrist James P. Comer (2005) developed a collaborative family engagement model composed of administrators, teachers, staff, and multidiverse parents/guardians empowered to support students' sense of safety, belonging, value, and competence. We suggest that schools implement a similar management model (which we call a Working Group) to support, analyze, and strengthen a school's or district's efforts to implement identity safety at home and school.

While many schools have parents and guardians who seem to naturally gravitate to being involved with us (and we appreciate their involvement), we must be vigilant in supporting multidiverse members to partner with us. Indeed, just as we want all students to be empowered, we want the same for parents/guardians, especially the ones who have been reluctant or may feel disconnected from joining us. As such, the process of determining the makeup and goals of a Working Group requires that we draw from the rich diversity of our school community. Additionally, it requires that we create mutually beneficial relationships rather than hierarchical ones.

The purpose of the Working Group is three-fold as seen in Figure 1.2.

Working Groups perform several essential functions including assessing the needs of the community, creating short- and long-term goals for achieving these goals and developing a strategic plan for creating an identity safe school environment that meets the needs of all students socially, emotionally, and academically.

Figure 1.2. Purpose of a Working Group

Reflection Task

Whether we form a new Working Group or incorporate the involvement of multidiverse parents/guardians in an existing leadership body, here are a few considerations:

- How can we provide outreach and facilitate the active involvement of parents/guardians from a wide range of backgrounds (e.g., parents who speak a language other than English)?
- How can we create identity safe spaces for parents/guardians that draw on their assets, offer a sense of belonging, and are validating of them?
- How can we support parents'/guardians' understanding of the school's mission and vision, policies, and practices?
- How can the school help families access after-school activities and additional community resources such as health and well-being care?

Educators and parents/guardians can share successes and challenges and ask essential questions of each other as they work to foster pride and embrace diversity among all children.

Positively Countering Opposition

Many schools have faced and continue to experience opposition from people who claim that teaching about diversity is akin to indoctrination. They point to critical race theory (CRT) as the culprit even though it represents an academic body of research that spans four decades, posits that race is a social construct, and that racism results from biased relationships and institutionalized laws and policies that can be positively disrupted to advantage all (not some) races or ethnicities (Editors of Encyclopedia Britannica, n.d.). Until recently, most K–12 educators were unaware of CRT and the depth of research behind it (Sawchuk, 2021). There is also a large body of research in the areas of culturally responsive or sustaining practices (also known as multicultural education) that demonstrates the efficacy of drawing from the diverse cultures found within our schools and society itself (Banks, 1997; Ladson-Billings, 1995; Zacarian & Soto, 2020). Identity safe teaching actively works to end bias and discrimination through culturally sustaining practices. It by no means is indoctrination!

Further, when parents/guardians approach us about CRT and identity safety as well as practices related to multidiversity, some may genuinely fear for their children. Others may be influenced (implicitly or explicitly) by media reports or even direct contact with groups who urge them to call the school and attend school board meetings to protest such practices as indoctrination and "unAmerican." We strongly suggest a proactive stance of meeting with groups of parents and students and collective language to appeal to our shared humanity. It is helpful to explain:

1. Every child has the right to learn.
2. Identity safe teaching creates spaces where students of all backgrounds are valued and included and all forms of bias are addressed.
3. Policies seek to advantage all students as members of a school community.
4. Labeling anyone as a racist or engaging in any form of name-calling is unacceptable.
5. Resolving inequities happens through raising awareness, leading to positive action rather than guilt or blame. It allows everyone to work for inclusion and justice. We progress through critical dialogues that reflect multiple perspectives while seeking equitable solutions.
6. Lessons on diversity promote pride in one's identity and background, benefitting students of all backgrounds.

Introducing Identity Safety to Students, Staff, and Families

Here are a few tips for introducing the concept of identity safety to children of various ages and staff and parents/guardians.

With younger children, you might say:

Each of us is unique and special. While everyone is different, we also have many things in common. When we are identity safe, everyone is happy to be themselves, and we can grow, learn, and play together.

With older students and adults, start with a metaphor:

Imagine you are the victim of identity theft. How would it feel to have someone steal your identity? You cannot get money from your bank account. You cannot function. Now, imagine someone stole your entire identity. You cannot be yourself. Maybe they did it by disparaging people who share your language, ethnicity, or gender identity. Maybe they just ignore you or mistreat you. How would that feel?

In an identity safe space, you can be your authentic self; you do not need to hide or leave your identity at the door.

Reflection Task

Describe how you might teach about identity safety:

To students:
To staff:
To parents/guardians:

After initially introducing the concept of identity safety to families, school leaders can continue the process by identifying:

- strengths and assets at home, school, and in the larger community;
- areas for strengthening policy, structures, practices, or professional development to support the inclusion of all children; and
- strategic short- and long-term plans to give all children a sense of safety, belonging, value, and competence.

LOOKING AHEAD

In this chapter, we introduced the SISP research and foundations of identity safety and explained why it matters. We discussed the negative impact of othering, colorblindness, and stereotype threat and how identity safety serves as an antidote to these hindrances to student learning and well-being. We also presented the importance of embracing diversity by actively noticing and listening, fostering pride, and building partnerships between home and school. We showed how this book breaks new ground for home and school partnerships where every child's identity safety is validated and fostered. In Chapter 2, we set the stage for creating an identity safe school by creating a caring and compassionate school culture.

ADDITIONAL RESOURCES

- **Stereotype Threat**
  - » C. Steele, How Stereotypes Affect Us and What We Can Do. https://www.youtube.com/watch?v=KvLj3OIQHuE
  - » Not in Our Town, Stereotype Threat: A Conversation with Claude Steele. https://www.niot.org/nios-video/stereotype-threat-conversation-claude-steele
  - » Steele, C. M. (2011). *Whistling Vivaldi: How stereotypes affect us and what we can do.* W. W. Norton & Company.

- **Identity Safety**
  - » Steele, D. M., & Cohn-Vargas, B. (2013). *Identity safe classrooms, K–5: Places to Belong and Learn*. Corwin.
  - » Cohn-Vargas, B., Kahn, A. C., & Epstein, A. (2021). *Identity safe classrooms, grades 6–12: Pathways to belonging and learning*. Corwin.

CHAPTER 2

Creating a Culture of Caring

When Francisco Lopes was 12 years old, his family moved from Santiago, Brazil, to a small college community in western Massachusetts where his father began working as a professor of Portuguese. Accompanied by his parents, Francisco enrolled in his new middle school, where his father enacted the role of family interpreter. Francisco and his parents are greeted in English by the school's receptionist, who smiles and, in English, points to some seats and asks them to wait for the school principal. Francisco's father stands when the principal, Mr. Murtaugh, greets the family in English, graciously takes their coats, hangs them in the office closet, and takes them on a tour of the school building. Principal Murtaugh shows the family the school's classrooms, cafeteria, and library and where Francisco's locker will be located. The family smiles politely throughout the tour experience, and Francisco's father listens carefully to Mr. Murtaugh's description of the school. The tour concludes with Principal Murtaugh shaking Francisco's and his father's hands and nodding politely at his mother. Then, Francisco participates in language testing with an English-speaking assessor to determine if he requires the school's English language education programming. While this short 10-minute assessment occurs, Francisco's mother waits quietly in the same seat in the school office, and his father leaves for work. After the testing session, Principal Murtaugh tries to speak with Francisco and his mother to tell them that Francisco qualifies for the language assistance program. He listens, and his mother nods, not really understanding what is being conveyed, and then they return home.

After the meeting, Principal Murtaugh meets with Francisco's team of teachers, including the ESL teacher assigned to his building. During their interaction, he shares that Francisco is a native Portuguese speaker from Santiago, Brazil, at the entering level of learning English and that he found the family to be very polite as he took them on a tour of the school to show them the various classrooms and "lay of the school." He also shares that Francisco will be enrolled in the ESL class for its half-hour daily period and the 7th-grade team.

On the first day of classes, Francisco becomes hopelessly lost. Hearing a cacophony of sounds in a language he does not understand and unsure where his classrooms, locker, or anything is in the building, he pulls his cell phone out of his pants pocket and calls his mother. "Please come get me!" he implores. His mother grabs her keys and hurriedly drives to the school, where Francisco anxiously waits for her to rescue him from the painful experience.

When his father arrives home from work and asks how Francisco's first day of school went, Francisco and his mother are afraid to tell his father the truth for fear of disappointing his choice to move the family so far from home. Throughout the rest of the week, Francisco continues to go to school for a short while and calls his mother to take him home. While this is occurring, neither Principal Murtaugh nor his teachers have any idea that Francisco is missing the first week of classes. It is not until the end of the week that Francisco and his mother tell his father what is occurring. Armed with this information, the whole family returns to the middle school to meet with Principal Murtaugh to see what can be done to ensure that Francisco is welcomed into his new school community.

In this chapter, we explore some of the key foundations for building a culture of trust and compassion and why it matters in the ever-changing landscape of our schools. Laying the groundwork of trust in a caring school environment sets the stage for fostering identity safety for students. From there, we can help parents/guardians support their children's identity safety at home. As such, we explore:

- What is a culture of trust, and why does it matter?
- What do we mean by culture and culture as a way of being and acting?
- Child development as an ever-growing, expanding, interactional process.
- The urgency for moving from a deficit to an asset-based approach.
- Partnerships between home and school.

Further, as in each chapter in our book, we will engage in reflection tasks throughout the chapter to help us examine the positive possibilities in sustaining a culture of trust, compassion, and cooperation as individuals, partners, small groups, and a whole system.

                      Reflection Task

Let us begin with a reflection task that looks back at the experience when Principal Murtaugh engaged Francisco and his parents. As with all the tasks in this book, this can be completed individually or with a partner, small group, or whole class as part of a professional growth or course experience.

1. Describe 2–3 activities that Principal Murtaugh engaged in to support Francisco and his family to feel welcomed and identity safe in his new school. Be as descriptive and detailed as possible.
2. What additional 2–3 activities would you have liked Principal Murtaugh to have done to ensure that Francisco was welcomed into his school? Again, be as descriptive and detailed as possible.
3. How do the activities that you listed account for Francisco's home language and culture?

WHAT IS A CULTURE OF TRUST AND CARING, AND WHY DOES IT MATTER?

In our last chapter, we delved into the theoretical underpinnings of identity safety. One of the key ideas we presented is that identity formation occurs in a social context (Markus et al., 2000). Identity safety occurs when certain conditions are present. At the opening of our chapter, we present our focal student, Francisco. He felt compelled to leave his school. We might argue reasonably that the fundamental reasons for Francisco's actions were the absence of his feeling safe, a sense of belonging, acknowledgment, and competence and that the omnipresence of these feelings compelled him to flee his new school. For many of us who are scholars in the underpinnings of culture as a way of being and acting, we know that we must look closely at what constitutes a culture of trust and care so that we can build and sustain a school community and support a home environment in which children unconditionally feel these conditions.

WHAT DO WE MEAN BY CULTURE AND CULTURAL WAY OF BEING?

In this book and many we have written, the terms "culture" and "cultural way of being" are used interchangeably to refer to two groups of children, families, educators, and others. These include those who are (1) from the dominant group of community members and (2) from an underrepresented group or groups of community members. While there are many definitions for the term culture, we draw from Trueba et al. (1981). They define culture and cultural way of being as "a form of communication with learned and shared, explicit, and implicit rules for perceiving, believing, evaluating, and acting. . . . What people talk about and are specific about, such as traditional customs and laws" (pp. 4–5). If we return to Francisco and his entrée into his new school in a new country, it gives us a glimpse of what we mean by the definition. In the example, Francisco listens to a language he cannot make meaning of while being situated in a location with which he has no familiarity.

In Chapter 1, we introduced the notion that every child needs support to navigate and negotiate myriad messages. We also stated that a child's sense of identity safety could be more firmly anchored when we create what we call a safe harbor for a child to feel the sense of safety, belonging, acknowledgment, and competence that we want all students to feel. We also introduced the notion that it is much more than fostering a student's positive sense of self. In a significant way, developing a culture of caring requires a deeper understanding, curiosity about, and appreciation for our students, their families, and ourselves.

Shining a Light on Who We Are as Educators

In 1990, the research described the American public-school educator as White, middle-class, and monolingual English-speaking. We know that there are many educators of color who are from underrepresented groups, and we need to diversify the teaching force further. However, current research shows that the profession's demographics have not changed significantly since the 1990s (National Center for Education Statistics [NCES], 2018). What exacerbates these findings further is the reality that most faculty of teacher preparation programs are also White (NCES, 2020).

Our point in stating these findings is that our populace is changing at such a rapid rate that we may not be able to keep pace with the changes that are occurring as they are occurring. An example is the 76,000 Afghanis who were airlifted out of Afghanistan to the United States due to the Taliban taking over the country (Jordan, 2022). The children from this group have had personal, social, cultural, and life experiences distinct from ours, including those of us of Afghani descent who did not experience the stress of fleeing the country).

Additionally, an empirical review of 101 studies completed during the 22-year span between 1980 and 2002 found that most preservice educators preferred working with students like themselves (Hollins & Guzman, 2005). These findings, coupled with many educators reporting the feeling of being inadequate in working with diverse student populations (Heineke & Vera, 2022; Samson & Lesaux, 2015), call for us to urgently pay much more intentional focus and empathy toward our understanding of what it means to be an educator in today's dynamically changing classrooms.

Reflection Task

1. How do the findings we presented about today's educators resonate with your experience?
2. How do the findings we presented differ from your personal experience?

Who Are Our Students?

In addition to deepening our understanding of who we are as educators, we also must consider the barriers that many children have experienced, are experiencing, or might experience through what we described in our first chapter as othering, stereotype threat, and colorblind practices. In addition to these three phenomena, our profession is developing a keener awareness about the epic number of children

- who have experienced or are experiencing adverse childhood experiences in the form of abuse, neglect, or significant household challenge (such as a family member who suffers from substance abuse, incarceration, being abused, or a mental illness, and more (Child and Adolescent Health Measurement Initiative, 2017; Felitti et al., 1998);
- with interruptions to their education;
- experiencing poverty;
- whose first language is other than or in addition to English; and
- experience bullying and bias-based harassment.

According to the research on these phenomena before the global COVID-19 pandemic, almost half of U.S. children experienced one or more significant adversities (Bethell et al., 2017; National Survey of Children's Health, 2016–17). In addition to this alarming statistic are findings about the nation's multilingual learners. What do we mean by the term multilingual learners? Many terms and acronyms are used to describe the broad range of students that have learned or are learning two or more languages and cultures (Zacarian, 2023). These include English learners (ELs); English language learners (ELLs); emergent bilinguals, long-term English learners (LTELs); students with limited or interrupted formal education (SLIFE) and other such terms. The term multilingual learner is growing widely in the field to affirm the linguistic assets that such students possess. We use this term in our book to reflect this broad population from the same strengths-based view.

Many multilingual learners have experienced:

> living in war and conflict zones; being persecuted in their home countries; being displaced, the long, arduous, and perilous trip to perceived safety in the United States; being separated from families; being inhumanely treated in detention centers; and living in constant fear of being deported and becoming homeless. (Zacarian et al., 2021, p. 47)

While some multilingual learners, such as Francisco, have had consistent prior literacy and academic learning experiences (Zacarian, 2013; Zacarian & Soto, 2020), many have had significant interruptions to education, including those who come to the United States for their first exposure to literacy and subject-matter learning (Calderón, 2007). Further, while 75% of this group are Spanish speaking, 2% are Arabic, 2% are Chinese, and 2% are Vietnamese, there are 400 different languages spoken amongst the nation's multilingual learners (U.S. Department of Education, n.d.-c). Further, the primary language one speaks is another factor.

> For example, students who speak Spanish have distinct cultures and represent many countries in Central and South America, others are from Caribbean nations, and many others were born in the United States. (Zacarian, 2023, p. 9)

A third and equally important reality is that an alarming number of the nation's total student population lived in poverty before the pandemic. For example, the poverty level for multilingual learners was disproportionately higher than all other groups (Southern Education Foundation, 2015), *and* they were far more likely to attend socioeconomically segregated schools with few resources (Quintero & Hansen, 2021). The COVID-19 pandemic exacerbated these realities to a much more intense degree.

In Chapter 1, we highlighted the devastating impact of discriminatory attitudes and bullying on LGBTQ+ students. In addition to the impact of race, ethnicity, and poverty, a recent national youth survey revealed that 19.5% of high school students had experienced bullying at school (Centers for Disease Control and Prevention, 2021). Even more alarming, between 2009 and 2019, there was a 44% increase showing that approximately one in six students reported making a suicide plan.

TAKING ACTION

All these realities urgently require us to think more deeply about what is needed to create more effective identity safe spaces. As you read this second example, look closely at how the school principal, Mr. Lahey, and the school community welcome student Tomás and his family.

Shining a Light on Giving Support to a Newcomer

Accompanied by his parents, Tomás enrolls in his new middle school, where his father enacts the role of family interpreter. As they enter the school office, they are warmly welcomed by the school receptionist, Mrs. Torres, who is bilingual in Portuguese and English. As they wait for Principal Lahey, Mrs. Torres asks them where they are from and what brought them to their town. Tomás and his parents share the reasons for moving. She comments politely on how exciting it is that Tomás's father is starting a new job at an accounting firm and asks Tomás about his prior school, including the activities he likes to participate in (soccer) and classes he likes (math). Tomás's father smiles broadly when the principal, Mr. Lahey, greets the family in English, graciously takes their coats, and hangs them in the office closet. Then, he asks the school receptionist, Mrs. Torres, to join them on a tour of the school building.

As Principal Lahey shows the family the school's classrooms, cafeteria, and library and where Tomás's locker will be located, he asks Tomás to describe what his prior school looked like. Then, with the support of Mrs. Torres, they exchange in a back-and-forth interaction about what is the same and different between his new middle school and his old one. The tour concludes with Principal Lahey and Mrs. Torres sharing that Tomás will be given an assessment in English to help determine the type of language assistance program that will be provided to support his learning of English and subject matter. Tomás and his parents ask some questions about the assessment, and Mrs. Torres and Principal Lahey respond to each of these. When they return to the office, they also discuss the school calendar and ask Tomás to share the start and end times of his old school. They carefully review the calendar with Tomás and his family, so they are well-informed of this information. They also confirm his address and support his and his family's awareness about the pickup and drop off location and time of the school bus to ensure that the family knows when and how Tomás will come to school. When this interaction is complete, Tomás is greeted by the language assessor, and the school receptionist Torres explains what Tomás will do during his short time with the assessor.

While this assessment ensues, Tomás's mother waits in the front office and his father leaves for work. Mrs. Torres asks Tomás's mother how families participated at Tomás's prior school, and then she shares activities that families engage in at the middle school. In addition, she shares information about the district's family liaison and interpreting services and various parent groups that she hopes Tomás's parents might join. After Tomás's language assessment, and with the interpretation of Mrs. Torres, Principal Lahey speaks with Tomás and his mother about the language assistance program and the 7th-grade team at the middle school. He also asks Tomás if he would like to have a buddy during the first weeks of school. Tomás enthusiastically agrees.

After the meeting, Principal Lahey meets with Tomás's team of teachers, including the ESL teacher assigned to his building. During their interaction, he shares what he has learned about Tomás and his family and excitedly tells them about his love of soccer and mathematics. Finally, the group of teachers and Principal Lahey collectively discuss the opening steps that will occur for Tomás. These include a former multilingual learner who will meet Tomás at the front door the next day and buddy with him during the first weeks of school.

 Reflection Task

Reflect on the activities Principal Lahey engaged in with Tomás and his parents.

1. Describe 2–3 activities Principal Lahey did to support Tomás and his family to feel welcomed to the middle school. Be as descriptive and detailed as possible.
2. What additional 2–3 activities would you include to ensure that Tomás felt welcomed to his new school? Again, be as descriptive and detailed as possible.
3. How do the activities that Principal Lahey did and you added account for Tomás's home language and culture?

CHILD DEVELOPMENT AS AN EVER-GROWING, EXPANDING, INTERACTIONAL PROCESS

One of the greatest differences between the two examples we presented in this chapter is the number of interactions that occurred among and between

1. Francisco, his parents, Principal Murtaugh in the first example at the opening of our chapter, and
2. the interactions that occurred between Tomás, his parents, the school's bilingual receptionist, Mrs. Torres, and Principal Lahey.

In the second example, the number of interactions that occurred greatly supported Tomás and his family's welcome into their new school community. A key reason for this support is that positive welcoming interactions (and lots of them!) play a critical role in a child's development, as do the partnerships we build with our school, family, and local communities on behalf of a child's success.

Renowned developmental psychologist Lev Vygotsky's (1978) contributions to what we know about learning affirm the significant role that interactions play in a child's development. He posited that children learn through two processes—cognition and social interaction. Indeed, children make meaning of the world around them by combining what they already know and have experienced with the interactions that they have with others, including all they encounter throughout their lives. Further, the ever-growing, ever-expanding circles of interactions greatly influence a child's identity and their positive (or negative) sense of self. If we return to the first example at the opening of our chapter, Principal Mr. Murtaugh did all the talking in a language Francisco did not comprehend. In a real sense, Principal Murtaugh engaged in a friendly monologue where he dominated the conversation. While Francisco's father engaged a little bit, and we might say they held a small dialogue between two of the people in this four-person group, what is needed is what we refer to as an "our-o-logue" where every member feels and is empowered to speak (Zacarian, 2023; Zacarian & Silverstone, 2020). In a real sense, we can see how Francisco was deprived of this urgently needed component—interaction. We certainly do not want to do that, and it is likely that neither did Mr. Murtaugh! Culturally responsive identity safe practices require supporting personally relevant and meaningful narratives between and amongst our students and their families (Zacarian & Silverstone, 2020). It also requires that we develop a deeper understanding of culture as a way of being and acting that is actualized through a child's interactions with us and others.

Mary Gauvain (2001, 2013), a seminal developmental psychologist, has significantly contributed to our understanding of the role that interaction plays in a child's development. Let us consider the example of a child at birth. The first people that the child meets are their parents or guardians. Whether it is two parents, single-parent, grandparent, foster parent, aunt, uncle, institutional caregiver, sibling, or another person who cares for the infant, it is their "consistent, routine, predictable, nurturing, and stimulating interactions" that support the child's development (Zacarian, Alvarez-Ortiz, & Haynes, 2017, p. 21). An example is when an infant cries. We can easily visualize a parent or guardian comforting the infant with food, a change to a dry diaper, or a hug. As the infant develops, their social world grows to include interactive encounters with their family's community, including their neighbors, markets the family shops, religious institutions the family attends, and much more. As depicted in Figure 2.1, by the time a child enrolls in our schools, they typically have 5 years of rich, supported, encouraged, and meaningful interactions amongst an ever-growing, ever-expanding circle of people. An example of the type of positive encounter we are referring to is a toddler who tumbles and falls and is immediately comforted by a parent or guardian, sibling, neighbor, or another person who shows that they care for and about the child's well-being.

Our example of the toddler tumbling and falling and being attended to by a caring individual highlights the importance of supportive and positive interactions. Further, these types of compassionate interactions demonstrate a sense of caring for and about our children as we want every community to do—including our family, school, local communities, and beyond. As such, by the time children come to us at the typical age of 5 years old, we are expected to care for and about the child in the same compassionate ways as they have been reared by their parents and guardians, family, and family communities (Zacarian, Alvarez-Ortiz, & Haynes, 2017; Zacarian & Silverstone, 2020).

Figure 2.1. Circles of Interaction

Note: Reprinted from Zacarian, D., Alvarez-Ortiz, L., & Haynes, J. (2017). *Teaching to strengths: Supporting students living with trauma, violence, and chronic stress.* ASCD.

Having stated this, one of the areas that we should be most concerned about is the level of isolation and low or limited social interactions that many children experience. While the COVID-19 pandemic exacerbated the degree of isolation students experienced, many face "extreme barriers, challenges, and constraints of isolation" in ways that do not afford the type of rich interactions that all students need (Zacarian et al., 2021). This is particularly true for many multilingual learners, especially those who fear deportation or live in areas where they have little contact with others. Figure 2.2 illustrates the type of isolation that such a student experiences. Consider the example of a child who lives in chronic fear of being discovered by the U.S. Immigration Customs and Enforcement (ICE) agency and deported.

There is another type of isolation that some students experience. Consider the example we furnished in Chapter 1 of Vinnie. Vinnie felt isolated from his peers and lived in constant fear of them after being bullied for not fitting into stereotypical gender norms. He also lived in constant fear of the shame that he perceived he would experience if he told his parents that he was gay. As seen in Figure 2.3, the type of isolation that Vinnie experienced reflects an impacting type of isolation that can, at its most intense level, lead to feelings of hopelessness and helplessness.

Figure 2.2. Barriers, Challenges, and Constraints of Isolation

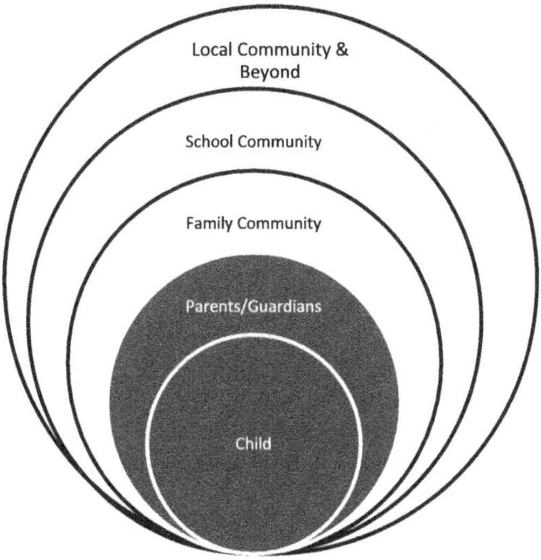

Note: Reprinted from Zacarian, D., Calderón, M. E., & Gottlieb, M. (2021). *Beyond crises: Overcoming linguistic and cultural inequities in communities, schools, and classrooms* (p. 48). Corwin.

Figure 2.3. Self-Imposed Isolation for Fear of Othering, Stereotype Threat, and More

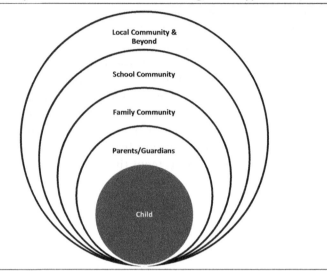

These different examples show us what can and does happen. However, rather than be discouraged or even feel powerless to help such students and their peers, we have great reason to be optimistic by understanding the importance of learning as a social–emotional process and our potential to build affirming and caring relationships with children.

Learning as a Social–Emotional Process

Educational scholars Costa (2017) and Kallick and Zmuda (2017) share the importance of building students' positive energy, engagement, and collaborations with others by our taking time to intentionally (1) build connections to their prior experiences, (2) draw from their current levels of expertise and competencies, and (3) spark students' interests, curiosities, and creativities. Further, they posit that learning is an emotional process that is taken in by all the senses. Therefore, to support the type of emotional excitement that they describe, we must be genuinely curious about our students by continuously expressing our interest in getting to know them on a personal level *and* taking time to connect their experiences and interests, as well as hopes and dreams, with what we teach. As such, learning is as much about whom we teach as it is what we teach.

This can only occur when we engage in a culture of caring for and about our children on a social and emotional level and when we take time to support students' assertiveness with and receptiveness toward others. Helping students develop this orientation does not happen by accident. As educators, we have a critical role in optimizing our students' social, emotional, and academic growth. It calls for us to help students learn to really listen to each other, express empathy for each other, pay attention to words and actions that they use with each other, mediate their emotions, and resolve the conflict in a productive manner (Zacarian & Silverstone, 2020). To do this, we must enact, model, and provide multiple and consistent practice opportunities for students to engage in interactions that fully and comprehensively support a culture of compassion and trust. However, first, we must understand the historical roots and urgency for moving from a deficit- to an assets-based stance.

The Urgency for Moving From a Deficits- to an Assets-Based Approach

Prior to the 1990s, the fields of psychiatry, psychology, social work, and education worked to identify and treat challenges. Commonly referred to as a deficits-based approach, we concentrated on identifying (or perceiving) what was wrong and finding remedies for it. Let us look at a dramatic example of this approach in action by returning to our first example of Francisco, in which he fled school, and he and his parents return for a second meeting to see what can be done.

Shining a Light on Supporting Multilingual Learners

As you read the example, consider how it shines a light on who we can be as educators when we do not promote a culture of compassion and trust by failing to engage with students in interactions and lots of them.

Weeks after the second meeting with the school principal, Mr. Murtaugh, Francisco continued to rarely engage in conversations with others. He also tended to get up from his desk and leave his classes and was found to rarely, if ever, be on-task in any of his classes. Rather than enact a multitiered system of support (MTSS) to support Francisco linguistically, academically, and socially–emotionally, a designee of the 7th-grade team of teachers met with the school's child study team. The meeting concluded with Francisco being referred for a special education evaluation. The evaluation was conducted entirely in English. The team determined that Francisco was significantly cognitively impaired and recommended that he be placed outside of the general classroom into a full day of special education programming. Astounded at these findings, his parents removed him from the school. Francisco and his mother returned to Santiago, Brazil, where they were separated from his father because they had found that "U.S. schools" were not for Francisco.

Reflection Task

Reflect on Francisco's experience.

1. How does Francisco's experience resonate or not resonate with your
    experience in a school setting?
2. What additional 2–3 activities would you have liked Francisco's 7th-grade
    team and the child study team to do to support Francisco? Again, be as
    descriptive and detailed as possible.
3. How do the activities that you listed account for Francisco's home
    language and culture?

If we look more closely at the type of approach that was used in this
opening chapter example, we can surmise that Francisco continues to be
and feel isolated and wholly unsupported in his new school setting. We
might also reasonably assume that Francisco's educators engaged in what
he was unable to do as opposed to what he could do and did not foster
a culture of compassion or trust. Research on this type of deficits-based
approach has shown that it has had little impact on improving students'
outcomes and, in fact, can and does support negative outcomes (Zacarian,
Alvarez-Ortiz, & Haynes, 2017; Zacarian & Silverstone, 2020). However,
we have great reason to think anew.

Research on the paramount need to shift our thinking to the assets and
strengths that all students, their families, and we possess has led to a historic transformation in the urgency for embracing and using a strengths-based
approach. Since the 1990s, researchers have affirmed the importance of
this approach. Seminal psychologist Abraham Maslow (1999) coined the
term *positive psychology* and the need to shift our focus to identifying "the assets, capacities, and qualities that empower people and their communities
to flourish" (Zacarian et al., 2017, p. 15). Positive psychology fully shifts
the focus from feeling helpless and hopeless in engaging others in positive
change to the possibilities that can be accomplished when we support individuals and groups to be the best version of themselves and support others
to do the same. It also adheres to creating a culture of compassion and
trust through fully operating and promoting a highly interactional schema
among and between students, their families, and our school and local community members and beyond. Education researchers Moll et al. (1992) affirm this vital shift. They researched families living on the border between
Mexico and the United States. While many who hold a deficit-based view
might describe the families who they researched as uneducated and, in kind,

unable to support their children with schoolwork, these researchers found the opposite. They observed that all the families possessed high levels of competencies and skills, what they referred to as *funds of knowledge*, at work and home and in rearing their children. As importantly, they also observed that the families passed these strengths and assets on to their children.

Over a decade later, Carol Dweck (2006), an internationally renowned psychologist and researcher at Stanford University, reported on the positives that can be demonstrated using a strengths-based approach. In her research, she looked closely at the different outcomes that occur when children are fully supported to see their and others' potential for growth. She asserts that there is a difference between having a hard and fast perception of ourselves and others (e.g., I am stupid in mathematics, I am incapable of learning algebra) versus a more open perception to our capacity to learn when we believe in ourselves and others. Dweck et al. (2014) coined the terms *fixed* versus *growth mindset*, arguing that encouraging the latter has been shown to have a far better chance of supporting students to succeed in school and in their lives. They also have contributed significantly to our seeing the positive possibilities of what can happen in communities with few resources. Namely, all students can experience greater success by using a strengths-based growth mindset.

Additionally, the shift in terminology from English Learner, English Language Learner, and Limited English Proficient to Emergent Bilingual and Multilingual Learner reflects this assets-based stance (Zacarian & Staehr Fenner, 2020). It does so by acknowledging, valuing, and honoring the many different languages and cultures that students and their families represent. As such, we have intentionally used the term multilingual learner throughout our book to reflect this assets-based stance.

The Power of Listening

Daniel is a college student whose parents are Guatemalan immigrants living in San Francisco. In his interview, we asked about aspects of his identity that matter to him; he explains:

> Two things that are true about me are that I'm a good listener and a good observer. More often than not, if I don't have to say anything, I won't. Whatever is appropriate for the current situation, or whatever it may be, or when somebody is on a rant or talking about something they're passionate about, you can see that sort of sparkle in their eyes. I'd say that's what I live for, to see somebody else talk about what they are passionate about. So therefore, I identify with listening—actively listening.

Like Daniel, adults and children can cultivate the capacity to listen actively. We teach young children to listen with their eyes, ears, and hearts, and we can do that ourselves. The identity safe teaching research identified the component "Listening to Student Voices" because when we can listen with our eyes to capture a person's emotional state, with our ears to hear their words, and with our hearts to feel empathy for them and what they are expressing. This noticing and listening helps us cultivate a culture of caring and compassion. When we use asset-based dialogue, highlighting strengths, people feel validated.

PARTNERSHIPS BETWEEN HOME AND SCHOOL

We can create a culture of caring and compassion by exercising these listening skills with adults in the school community, including staff and families. Also, we can help families develop listening skills with children at home. By noticing and listening, educators and families can recognize children's hopes, dreams, desires, and needs. With an asset-based approach, each child can feel that who they are, what they think, and how they feel matter (Cohn-Vargas et al., 2021). Additionally, when families feel heard, they are more likely to attend meetings and be our partners by offering ideas, questions, and concerns that fortify our working together.

All families possess rich personal, social, cultural, linguistic, and other resources that can greatly help us bring a unit of study alive (Zacarian, et al., 2015, 2020). An example is a chemistry teacher who is teaching a unit of study on thermal reactions. To illustrate the concepts, she invites a mother who is a welder at a local auto shop to demonstrate an authentic example of a thermal reaction. Personal and career connections such as this one, accompanied with cultural and linguistic connections, world experiences, and social connections, can empower families to be our partners. Another example is a parent who previously lived near the rainforest region in Brazil who comes to a kindergarten science class that is exploring the question: Why are rainforests important to our planet? Helpful strategies for doing this in K–12 include

- supporting parents/guardians to come to class by informing them in advance about what students are learning, the number of students in the class, and what students might ask during their visit; and
- having students welcome a parent/guardian to the class and later write a class thank you note for the contribution.

We can create identity safe spaces for parent/guardian participation by welcoming their voices in the classroom and by inviting their participation in school-based teams and, importantly, in leadership teams like our Working Group. We can do this by being responsive to families and providing resources they are entitled to, including translators and childcare. In Chapter 6, we offer additional types of activities to build school- and classroom-based partnerships with children's involvement.

Listening Tours: A Way to Gather Information and Connect With the Community

A "listening tour" is the process of meeting with an individual or group (e.g., a staff member, parent, or group of community partners who represent multidiverse identities and backgrounds) and actively listening to what is stated, observing their actions, and making connections through listening as opposed to speaking. For example, the goal of a listening tour might be to gather general information about how the person is feeling or receiving input on a topic (e.g., how they feel the curriculum is working or needs strengthening, the special education intake process). A listening tour can be done by one or more school leaders or a larger constituency, such as the identity safety Working Group we proposed in Chapter 1. The focus of this work is on listening carefully without judgment to learn about and become familiar with partners so that it is a mutually empowering endeavor. Listening tours and other forms of gathering input are a beginning step toward building and sustaining relationships. The intent is to gain deeper connections and build trusted partnership.

Shining a Light on Listening Tours

Former principal and superintendent Louise Bay Waters (2022) has been reflecting on her 50-year career focused on equity and antiracism. She shared her ideas in an essay entitled "Listening While White: Learning to Lead."

I have come far from my first days as a new teacher. Far enough to know the limitations of my listening skills and the bridges I still struggle to build. What I do know is that I cannot learn if I do not listen. And I cannot listen unless I create opportunities to hear, particularly from communities that are disconnected from schools by past experience, culture, or language. More painfully, I have learned that in order to listen, I must be willing to push through my own insecurities. While listening is a prerequisite for any leader, it is a critical skill when leading while White. It allowed me to find landmines and points of commonality and to begin to build trust. Allies I acquired then kept me apprised of hot topics, smoldering tensions, and opportunities.

As a mid-career elementary principal, some of the Afghan families that I worked with were refugees, while some came from the educated elite whose parents spoke English. Students from this latter group often outperformed their American peers, particularly in math. However, most who lived in refugee camps had limited access to schooling. The needs of each student were different, and that range was repeated in the other immigrant groups. Listening taught me to be wary of generalizations.

Through these initial listening tours and ongoing parent conversations, I discovered a sadness among many immigrant parents. They were proud of their children's growing English but alarmed at the loss of their native language. They worried that without the ability to communicate, they could not support their children academically. However, their deepest fear was losing their authority. How could they ensure their children respected the teacher? How could they protect them from drugs or gang activity if the children no longer respected them, their culture, or their language?

The opportunity to listen expanded greatly when we instituted a Language Academy offering primary language instruction in multiple languages. Previously few immigrant parents participated in school activities, and most were reluctant to interact with the school at all. At our fall festival, Language Academy parents ran food booths—biryani, pancit, and imperial rolls sold fast. The classes participated in the spring talent show, and their families attended. Now when teachers wanted to connect with parents, they were easy to find with translation readily available. I was able to build strong relationships with this quarter of our families, ones previously invisible in our school. The insights I gained through these interactions were invaluable in building a cohesive school community.

Structuring and Managing Listening Tours

In addition to individual meetings with school leaders, small groups of parents/guardians might collaborate with educators to hear their thoughts, hopes, and concerns and to inform a larger Working Group. For example, a small group representing a particular ethnicity or identity group can offer important insights that we might otherwise miss (e.g., Venezuelan immigrants, lesbian mothers, parents of students with autism).

Plan an agenda for the session. Generate a series of open-ended strengths-based questions to support the positive possibilities of partnerships (e.g., What are your hopes and dreams for your child? In what ways has your child flourished at this school? What ways can the school better serve your child's academic needs? What resources would help your family? What kinds of parent education activities would benefit you and your children?). Add targeted questions to explore a particular issue facing the school. For example, if there is a problem with bullying, you can ask if their child has experienced bullying and find out how the parent/guardian felt it was handled and if it was resolved.

At the close of the session, summarize what you have learned. For example, a small group may have discussed challenges that a particular group of students are experiencing, may suggest various ideas for remedying these challenges, and may make recommendations.

Thank the participants and tell them you will bring their ideas to your Working Group or leadership team. Also, be sure to follow-up and let them know of any changes that resulted from their suggestions.

Tips for Facilitating Multidiverse Parents/Guardians in Working Groups

Take time to plan carefully. This will help in having more productive sessions and avoid some of the common pitfalls that can occur when groups work together. Assign roles such as facilitator, timekeeper, note taker, so these are shared, and no one person is the sole leader. Share the responsibilities for these roles so that members clearly know what is expected when each is enacted.

> For example, the facilitator's role is to paraphrase what is stated to ensure that everyone is understood, ask clarifying questions as needed, and allow all points of view to be expressed. The timekeeper's role is to allot a certain period for a group discussion and to provide a 2- and 1-minute warning when the time is scheduled to end. Finally, the notetaker's role is to take careful notes of the group meeting and disseminate these within a specified time.

Also, plan how to rotate these roles so that everyone can participate actively in ways that are comfortable.

Know your community by taking time to develop relationships and build trust. Avoid making assumptions or stereotypes about any individual or group.

Be aware of different communication styles and ways of interacting. Be cognizant that different cultures approach time differently. Some insist on punctuality, and others are more flexible. Become acquainted with various preferences that participants have for working together. Secure a way to accommodate all of them. For example, a parent may prefer a translator to fully comprehend what is being communicated and be more comfortable speaking English with the group. Another parent may rarely speak at all and use body language to signal a response.

Become familiar and flexible with different forms of communication. People have different ways they interact: some use texts, some prefer phone calls, some prefer video calls, and some use email. Find out parents'/guardians' preferences. For example, some may be most comfortable using WhatsApp, a free messaging and video application. It is essential to be as flexible and open to ensure that the means of communication works with parents/guardians and is not a barrier. Secure translators to communicate with families and ensure a smooth and meaningful flow of back-and-forth communication with parents/guardians. This is a critical activity that schools are obligated to do as part of the laws and regulations governing the education of multilingual learners and families who are not yet able to communicate with us in English (U.S. Department of Justice and U.S. Department of Education, January 7, 2015).

Prepare a structured agenda with approximate times for each activity. Ensure time for input and to solicit opinions and ideas from participants and, as important, allot time for translations. Support the group in providing wait time for the flow of dialogue to be paced for interpreters to have time to share what has been stated and for parents/guardians to respond. Include a warm, welcoming activity to ensure every participant is acknowledged and honored. Take time for introductions and express gratitude for parents/guardians taking time from their busy lives to participate.

Stick to the agenda and use a "parking lot" to list topics that are not on the agenda for discussion at a future meeting.

Set goals: Identify goals for the meeting and short- and long-term goals for working together. Parents/guardians have a range of experiences meeting in groups in school settings, from those who are at the entering stage with no prior background to those at the proficient stage with years of experience. Set goals and make them visible using handouts or a whiteboard, just as we would do in classrooms, and participants can "see" what to expect. Include the overarching goal of what the group is expected to do (e.g., we will review the rules for student behavior in school) and the goal for the day's meeting (e.g., we will look at our attendance policy).

Introduce community agreements with norms for working together: By coming to an agreement at the outset, expectations for behavior are communicated regarding how everyone in the group will interact as they work together. If someone violates an agreement, they can simply be reminded by referring to the agreement to "listen respectfully" or "ensure everyone gets a chance to speak."

Incorporate strategies that allow everyone to participate: Start with a basic awareness of your audience and their needs. Be sure to have translation available for people who speak languages other than English to understand what is being said. If necessary, use a microphone and pass it around to ensure all participants can hear what is being said. Ask participants to raise their hand to speak and avoid speaking a second time until everyone who wishes to speak has a chance to do. If the meeting is on Zoom, set protocols for participation at the beginning (e.g., raise hands to speak, mute your microphone when not speaking).

Expect that there will be differences of opinion ranging from polite disagreement to an emotional response. In addition to reminding people of the norms, allow participants the opportunity to fully express their ideas without being interrupted. Ask speakers to elaborate on why they believe something is important. Ask others to share their perspective in a respectful manner and provide a model of what that looks like. (For example, "I hear Mrs. Katch say that her eldest child helps younger siblings get ready for school as she works the night shift. That sounds challenging. We might want to revisit our absentee policies to see how we can allow for these types of occurrences.")

Enjoy the collaboration process, express gratitude to participants for their participation, and celebrate the group's successes! We discuss ways to facilitate conversations about race and gender in Chapter 3.

Positively Countering Opposition

Some people claim that highlighting our differences will divide us, saying, "Wouldn't it be better if we wipe all differences away so we could be one happy family?" The answer is a resounding no! As we discussed in Chapter 1, if someone feels different or marginalized in some way, a colorblind environment can make that person feel invisible or lack belonging. Like the biodiversity of nature, an environment that treats differences as assets significantly strengthens the capacity to work together and solve problems. Here are some strategies to partner with parents and guardians:

1. Invite parents/guardians to meet or speak with you in person, by phone, or using video chat. Listen fully to their concerns.
2. Be curious, open, and flexible, and avoid being judgmental.
3. Ask for clarification (e.g., "What caused your child to feel this way?).
4. Offer to investigate and schedule a time to follow up with the parent.

5. Explain that when systemic inequities are found (such as any policy that unwittingly results in any form of oppression), remedies will be implemented.
6. When appropriate, cite teaching standards that include learning about the history of racism and sexism.
7. Close the conversation by highlighting efforts to ensure all students feel identity safe and have a sense of belonging. Acknowledge that learning about some historical inequalities is challenging. Assure the parent that you are committed to the school's mission to promote equity, diversity, and critical thinking.
8. Express gratitude for the parent's willingness to share their concerns. Ask if they have any additional ideas, concerns, or questions. Conclude the call with a hopeful message.

 Reflection Task

The following reflection activity can be done individually. It also can occur with groups of families. Ask participants to work in small groups to discuss the questions and prepare to share the key ideas with the whole group. Then, ask the whole group to listen to each other's ideas, questions, and concerns and identify actions to improve the school.

1. What are the ways our school creates a culture of caring?
2. How can our school enhance its culture of caring for students of all backgrounds?
3. What listening strategies have been used to build connections with families? What benefits might be gained from a listening tour?
4. How might parents/guardians be partners in new ways to enhance a school's culture?

LOOKING AHEAD

In this chapter, we explored the importance of a culture of trust. We also defined the concept of culture and culture as a way of being and acting. We shone a light on child development as an ever-growing, ever-expanding interactional process. We also explored the urgency for moving from a deficit- to an asset-based approach. Finally, we looked at ways to build home-school partnerships. In Chapter 3, we will examine the power of reflecting on our own identities in support of identity safety at school.

ADDITIONAL RESOURCES

- **From Nobody Cares to Everyone/Every Community Cares**
  Zacarian, D. & Dove, M. G. (2020). *From nobody cares to everyone/every community cares.* In M. E. Calderon, M. G. Dove, D. Staehr Fenner, M. Gottlieb, A. Honigsfeld, T. W. Singer, S. Slakk, I. Soto, and D. Zacarian (Eds.), *Breaking down the wall: Essential shifts for English learners' success* (pp. 183–200). Corwin.
- **Listening Tours**
  Cohn-Vargas, B., Kahn, A.C., Epstein, A., & Gogolewski, K. (2022). *Belonging and inclusion in identity safe schools: A guide for educational leaders* (pp. 55–56). Corwin.
- **What's the urgency for culturally responsive teaching?**
  Zacarian, D., & Soto, I. (2020). *Responsive schooling for culturally and linguistically diverse students* (pp. 1–24). Norton Education.

CHAPTER 3

Understanding Our Own Identity

Angela Ghent is a high school teacher of multilingual learners in South Carolina. Here is a summary of the steps she and her school principal take when a new student enrolls.

> The school's principal looks for the students at lunch to ensure they have friends to sit with. He notices their changes in behavior as they learn to speak more English and gives them public recognition and awards for their academic achievements. He sets the tone for teachers, counselors, and administrators to provide these students with a warm welcome and go the extra mile to meet their needs. (Zacarian & Silverstone, 2015, p. 88)

One of the first activities that Angela does with students is to help them to write a personal narrative for a teacher of their choice or the school principal. She explains that she does this because

> To borrow terms from literature class, newcomers who don't speak English have no voice. They are flat characters to their teachers. [However, when they] present personal narratives to their teachers and talk about themselves through writing, they become "round characters." (Zacarian & Silverstone, 2015, pp. 88–89)

One of us, Debbie, has used this example countless times across the country when providing professional development about building partnerships with and among culturally, racially, ethically, linguistically, and socioeconomically diverse students, their families, and members of a school and local community. Two of the two key questions explored are:

1. What are the values, beliefs, and perceptions that Angela and the school principal portray?
2. How are the values, beliefs, and perceptions that you have identified demonstrated in your workplace? Be as detailed as possible.

Thousands of educators have shared countless examples of the steps that they and colleagues have taken to support students' sense of safety, belonging, value, and competence. It has opened windows to discussing some of the complexities that inevitably occur when we work with *other people's children*—a term that scholar Lisa Delpit (2006) used and aptly titled her groundbreaking book *Other People's Children.*

We have observed many powerful examples of families seeking to create identity safety for their own children during our decades of working with them. The interviews that we conducted for this book provide many additional ones. For instance, we will meet Sonia later in this chapter and learn about the steps she took to support her transgender child.

In this chapter, we respond to the following questions:

- Why is it important to explore our own identities? Why does it matter?
- How can we examine our own implicit and explicit biases to support identity safe spaces?
- What steps can we take to build reflective home-school partnerships?

In Chapter 2, we presented demographic information about the nation's multidiverse student and family populations. In addition, a growing number of children

- are being raised by people other than their parents or live in foster homes;
- are experiencing adverse childhood experiences;
- have limited or interrupted formal literacy and academic experiences;
- live in poverty; and
- have been diagnosed with one or more disabilities.

We also shared that the dominant population of educators is White and middle class.

While these are essential factors to consider as we approach the complex topic of identity safety, we are *not saying* that all students, families, and teachers come from one or more of these groups. What we are saying is that wherever we work and whatever we do, it is important to be inclusive.

A powerful example of enacting the type of inclusionary stance that we are referring to can be found in the groundbreaking book *Far From the Tree: Parents, Children, and the Search for Identity* by Andrew Solomon (2012). Solomon explores the experiences of parents/guardians whose children are greatly different from themselves—including children who are transgender, deaf, prodigies, autistic, schizophrenic, and others. Throughout the book are examples of the meaning the parents/guardians derive in rearing their children. Books such as this one and our goal of being inclusive point to doing as much as possible to create and sustain identity safe spaces for children to thrive and for parents/guardians to be our partners.

In earlier chapters, we discussed the critical role that social interactions play in a child's identity development. What is also important is collaborating as partners on behalf of children. It furthers the point of our credo that *interactions, and lots of them,* are so critical!

Shining a Light on the Influence of Culture

Sonia was born in Canada after her parents immigrated from India. Sonia believes in the importance of her children interacting with the same cultural heritage as hers, especially because they are surrounded by peers who are different from them. Here is what Sonia states:

> My children have a lot of South Asian family friends that they have grown up with, pretty much like cousins. They have a huge community of aunties who are literally like second moms to them. Also, they're close to both of their grandparents, a source of joy and resilience for us. We're very culturally South Asian together, celebrating Diwali and other festivals. Our children study South Asian dance. Sheila (one of Sonia's children) performed and is the standout in her dance class.

Sonia believes in the benefits of engaging her children with a community who share the same cultural, linguistic, ethnic, and racial backgrounds.

Reflection Task

1. In what ways do Sonia's beliefs about being reared with cultural, linguistic, ethnic, and racial members of the same background resonate or not resonate with your childhood experiences? Be as detailed as possible.
2. Based on your response, how might you explain 1–2 beliefs and perceptions about the culture in which you were reared?

In Chapter 2, we discussed Mary Gauvain's (2013) research on the role that interactions play in a child's development. Indeed, a child's repeated exposure to the rituals and behaviors at home and in family communities becomes the glue that binds a cultural community together. Sonia's example of her children's experiences is an example of Gauvain's important finding.

Shining a Light on Our Positive Emotional Experiences

Another means to explore who we are as educators and parents/guardians is to consider our own personal experiences, our perceptions of them, and how these are tied to our beliefs about our children and learning. Let us look at one of us, Debbie, through her childhood experiences.

I (Debbie) was reared in a two-parent home. My mother came to the United States as a young child from Lithuania. She loved the ritual of going to the library every week and borrowing many books. She regularly brought me and my older sisters along to this weekly ritual. I vividly recall bringing as many books home from the children's section of the library and "reading" them as my mother did—even if it meant pretending to read each one.

Another childhood memory is my wanting to knit like my mother did. Being left-handed and my mother being right-handed led her to think she could not teach me how to do the craft. Not to be stopped from my goal of knitting, I went to the *World Book Encyclopedia*, looked up the word "knit" with a "k," snuck into my mother's bag of leftover balls of yarn, figured out how to knit from the hand-drawings in the encyclopedia, and knit a scarf. Though it was full of holes and mistakes, that scarf was a testament to what I believed was a feat of using reading to create a hand-knit piece. My reward was three-fold:

1. Praise from my family for my accomplishment.
2. My father wearing the hole-ridden scarf for years.
3. (Finally!) being taught to knit by a family friend who was completely blind. I vividly remember my knitting teacher using words to teach me the craft and her fingers to correct my errors and inspire me to do more.

Reflection Task

Consider our schema about identity safety and its relationship to positive interactions.

- How do you believe that Debbie's childhood reading and knitting experiences reflect what we have explored about identity safety and its relationship with positive interactions?

THE ROLE OF RITUALS COUPLED WITH
POSITIVE INTERACTIONS

Observing the same rituals over and over again contributes greatly to our understanding of the world around us, as do positive interactions and lots of them. For example, Debbie observed the rituals of reading and knitting, engaged in a myriad of positive emotional interactions about her desire to engage in these activities, and still does! Educational scholar Arthur Costa (2017) describes this type of positive learning experience as a wholly emotional one that is taken in through the senses and boosts our interest in learning.

It is important for us to understand development through Gauvain's lens of observing and interacting and learning through Costa's lens of emotions. Going back to the childhood example of learning how to knit, imagine if Debbie's family had an entirely negative reaction and punished her for "stealing" her mother's yarn. Those negative reactions might have led her in a very different developmental trajectory.

It calls on us to look at ourselves as individuals and the family, school, and local community in which we were reared to gain some insights as to who we are. Let's begin by looking at our own social identities.

 Reflection Task

Consider one or more than one childhood experience that influenced your identity.

1. Describe the experience(s).
2. Describe 1-2 ways that the experience(s) influenced who you are as an adult.
3. Describe how the influence of this experience (or experiences) is reflected in your identity as an educator.

As educators, it is critical for us to understand that our life experiences, that is, who we are as individuals and communities of people, can be vastly different from many of our individual students and groups of students. For example, we may find ourselves making the mistake of assuming that all our students are reared in homes that approximate ours. Not true! One example of a distinct home environment is Jesús, who was reared on the Texas-Mexico border.

Shining a Light on Differences in Home Environments

Jesús, his brothers, sisters, and parents lived in an old warehouse. Their family was separated by a blanket for privacy from another family who also lived in the warehouse. A few years later, his family moved to a one-room hovel in a town next to a cantina.

Jesús explains:

> The *migra* [border patrol] often drove through our neighborhood hunting for un-documented people. One indelible memory was when I was 5. My grandmother spied the truck through the window. She picked up my two brothers and me and ran out the door tossing us into the brush behind the cantina to hide.

Reflection Task

Consider Jesús's childhood home and life experience.

1. In what ways was Jesús's childhood home environment the same as or different from yours? Be as detailed as possible.
2. In Chapter 2, we presented the importance of using an assets-based approach. One strength is the action that Jesús's grandmother took to protect Jesús and his brother from being apprehended by the border patrol. Identify another strength that Jesús experienced.

Additionally, the differences between students and families from collectivist versus individualistic cultures are important to consider. In collectivist culture, group harmony is highly valued, and cooperation is a foundational natural part of family and community life (DeCapua & Marshall, 2010; Hofstede, 2011; Hofstede et al., 2005; Tyler et al., 2008). In individualistic cultures, including dominant western European countries and the United States, competition and individualism are ways of being and acting (DeCapua & Marshall, 2010; Hofstede, 2011; Hofstede et al., 2005; Tyler et al., 2008). While we will discuss this in more detail in Chapter 6, the following example illustrates our point.

Shining a Light on Cultures That Value Interdependence

Interdependence is a way of life for Paula Rabideaux, an educator we met in Chapter 1. She explains she is the mother of four. She grew up on the Menominee

Reservation, the home of many generations of her family. As you read this segment, consider your experiences with collaboration and competition in your family and at school.

> An example of our value of interdependence happened when my son was in eighth grade. He came home one day saying, "I think I upset my teacher. She called on me because she knew I had the answer but wouldn't say it. I think I disappointed her because I didn't respond."
>
> So, I asked, "If you knew the answer, why didn't you respond?"
>
> He replied, "Well, she looked right at me, making me uncomfortable. My friend was sitting next to me. When she asked the question, I could see him scooting down in his seat, distressed because he didn't know the answer. I felt terrible because he isn't a strong student and has difficulty learning. He's a good person but needs a lot of help. I didn't want him to feel worse, so I didn't answer in front of him." Then my son asked, "Please talk with the teacher to explain what happened. I don't think she understands the differences, and I don't want to seem like I'm boasting or showing off."
>
> When teachers understand cultural differences, they can help students learn to navigate the two worlds without sacrificing their way of being.
>
> (Cohn-Vargas & Rabideaux, 2023, pp. 42–43)

 Reflection Task

1. How does Paula's example resonate or not resonate with your childhood experiences?
2. How might your experience influence the response you might give to a student who is hesitant to respond to a question?

In addition to the example we just furnished, consider the enormous number of children exposed to one or more adverse childhood experiences that can and do powerfully affect their lives. The unique and unpredictable nature of abuse, neglect, and/or household challenges that they experience may have little connection to our own life experiences. As a result, we may have little reference from which to draw. This is particularly true for individuals and groups of people who experience the phenomena of racial trauma.

UNDERSTANDING THE PHENOMENA OF RACIAL TRAUMA
IN ADDITION TO ADVERSE CHILDHOOD EXPERIENCES

As we seek to support a child's positive identity development and understand Gauvain's and Costa's contributions, we must pay just as much, if not more, attention to the negative impacts that an overwhelming number of children routinely encounter. These include what sociologist Kenneth Hardy (2013) refers to as *racial trauma* in the form "of interpersonal violence that can lacerate the spirit, scar the soul, and puncture the psyche" (p. 25). Unlike the type of adverse childhood experiences that we defined in Chapter 2 regarding abuse, neglect, and household challenges, Hardy describes racial trauma as the manifestation of repeated experiences devaluing a person's race and sense of self. Further, he posits that racial trauma is experienced as an onslaught of messages that support children in seeing themselves as "not as attractive as . . . not as smart as . . . too dumb to . . . not intelligent enough to . . . not college material . . . not welcomed here, and so forth" (p. 26). Further, Hardy explains that racial trauma can lead to *internalized devaluation* by repeated exposure to a cascade of continuously negative observations and/or interactions that lead to a traumatic response, lack of worthiness and value, as well as *voicelessness*. Racial trauma also can inhibit a person's capacity to advocate for themselves and be persistent because failure is a perceived certainty. Tragically, like water continuously dripping on a rock, racial trauma can erode confidence and explode into what Hardy calls "a wound of rage" and resentment (p. 26).

Here is an example of the type of explosion Hardy is referring to. It comes from an adult, Lori, who recalls a traumatic childhood experience.

Shining a Light on Our Experiences With Racial Trauma

As you read the interview segment from Lori, an African American engineer with two children, consider how it reflects or does not reflect your own experience.

I'm a little 4-year-old girl, and we've just moved into our new house. Things have not been going well with the neighbors. (We didn't have any problems with the neighbors initially. As a matter of fact, my little brother and Peggy became best friends.) A little neighbor girl comes over. She's probably about 2-and-a-half, and she calls me the N-word. My reaction was that I picked up a big piece of blacktop from the crumbling driveway and hurled it at her. It hit her in the eye, and she ran into her house. I ran the other way because I knew I was in trouble. My father came out and asked, "Did you throw a rock at Peggy?"

I replied, "She called me nigger." My parents didn't punish me for throwing the rock at Peggy, but I didn't really understand what happened. Now, looking back on it as an adult, I imagine that I must have been called that word a lot in my young mind for me to have such a violent reaction, especially when my mind was too young to understand what was happening. That was my first introduction and reaction to racism. And I've pretty much been dealing with it ever since.

Reflection Task

1. Explain Lori's reaction by revisiting what we have explored about racial trauma.
2. How does Lori's childhood recollection resonate or not resonate with your childhood experiences? Be as detailed as possible.

We believe that racial trauma can be applied to many underrepresented individuals and groups, including Latinx, Indigenous Americans, Asian, LGBTQ+, poor, and others. These realities call for us to examine and reexamine our implicit and explicit biases so that we may create and enact identity safe spaces for our students and mutually meaningful partnerships with their families.

HOW CAN WE EXAMINE OUR OWN IMPLICIT AND EXPLICIT BIASES TO SUPPORT IDENTITY SAFE SPACES?

Our beliefs influence our interactions and shape who we are as individuals. We all have biased attitudes toward or against people, places, or things. These learned associations are shaped by our experiences. Implicit bias occurs unconsciously and causes us to react, sometimes even before we have time to think. These biases may be buried deep in our unconscious mind and even be counter to our conscious beliefs. We are all subject to implicit biases about others and even our own identities.

For example, in one study, participants were asked to evaluate the résumés of candidates applying for a university position. The exact résumé was given to participants with one difference. Some participants received a version of the résumé attributed to a female, while others saw that same résumé with a male name. Results showed that male and female study participants were more willing to hire male candidates and rated the males higher for teaching, research, and service (Steinpreis et al., 1999).

Since stereotyping about gender, race, and other differences is the norm in society, implicit biases can lead to harmful and devastating results. Examples of this range from paying women less than males doing the same jobs (Iacurci, 2022) to a policeman shooting an unarmed Black person when he mistakenly thought he saw a gun (Eberhardt et al., 2004). Here are a few school-based examples of implicit bias that we heard during our interviews:

- Repeatedly forgetting to use a student's preferred gender pronoun
- Placing students of color in lower-level courses
- Mispronouncing a student's name
- Confusing and mixing up the names of two students of the same ethnicity
- Suspending and expelling Black students at rates higher than White students for the same behaviors

Although implicit bias occurs at the unconscious level, researchers have demonstrated that it can be reduced. For example, in an 8-week intervention, social psychologist Patricia Devine et al. (2012) reduced implicit bias through the following practices:

Individuation: Looking at people as individuals instead of judging a whole group.

Empathetic perspective taking: Learning to appreciate another person's point of view.

Countering stereotypic images: Deconstructing and refuting negative stereotypes that feed into unconscious attitudes (e.g., Black boys wearing hoods are dangerous, Black and Latinx students are not college material, etc.).

Shining a Light on Our Beliefs

Consider the following example from Sonia, a university professor and mother we met earlier. One day during the school year, Sonia's 6-year-old child, assigned male at birth, declared:

"*Mom, I'm a girl.*"

In response to her child's declaration, Sonia thought the following: *It was as if my child was saying, I'm here, I'm just telling you.*

Reflection Task

Consider Sonia's situation and imagine if it had happened to you.

- How might you react if you were this child's parent?
- Based on your response, how might you explain your reaction?

Citing the U.S. Department of Education's mission, Gullo et al. (2018) affirm that "Schools need to equip all students, regardless of race, ethnicity, gender, or ability status—with the opportunities and skills necessary to reach their potential" (p. 4). Despite our best intentions at the local, state, and national levels, we all too often negate our commitment to be inclusive (Greenwald et al., 2002; Kawakami & Miura, 2014).

Positively Countering Opposition

A helpful way to consider the type of unconscious and conscious bias that these scholars are referring to is to look through the lens of an interview that was conducted by Audie Cornish, a nationally recognized, award-winning anchor and correspondent for *CNN News* and former NPR co-host of the popular news show *All Things Considered*. Cornish launched a new podcast, *The Assignment*. The podcast consists of interviews with people from headline news. On November 17, 2022, Cornish interviewed two conservative parent activists from Duvall, Florida, and Lansing, Michigan, who ran for and won positions on their local school boards. At the opening of the interview, the two activists share that they ran for political office because they were concerned about school closures during the pandemic, the way gender identity is taught in schools, and how schools "handled issues of race and diversity as a code word for being anti-white" (Cornish, 2022). During a portion of the interview, Cornish plays a brief segment of Governor Ron DeSantis's speech at the "Moms for Liberty" summit in July 2022 in which DeSantis states:

> In the state of Florida, a parent should be able to send their kid to kindergarten without having "woke gender ideology" shoved down their throat. We're not going to have some first grader be told that your parents named you Johnny, you were born a boy, but maybe you're really a girl. (Cornish, 2022)

After playing the segment from DeSantis's speech, Cornish then poses the following question:

What's your response to that [statement of Governor DeSantis]? I'll start with you, April because you were among the [Florida] candidates that he supported. (Cornish, 2022)

April Carney's response:

I think a five-year-old who still believes in Santa Claus and the Easter Bunny doesn't need to be taught about gender ideology. I think once you go through puberty and you start to figure out who you are and your hormones begin to even out, then yeah. If that's how you're feeling, and if it were my child, I'd be completely accepting of that child. But at that age, it's not necessary in the classroom. House Bill 1557 is about age-appropriate curriculum. Not one place in that bill doesn't mention anything about singling out children for their, you know, persuasion. (Cornish, 2022)

 Reflection Task

Let's imagine that newly elected school board member April Carney is working amongst like-minded school board members where you work as an elementary school educator. The school board orders new district policies to be issued immediately in your workplace, requiring all elementary school administrators, teachers, and support staff not to speak about a child's gender identity. In this hypothetical scenario, a child comes to your school no longer dressing as a typical boy. He is now clad in pink dresses and declares himself to be a girl. You observe some of his classmates ridiculing his choice of apparel and calling him a liar for claiming he was a girl when they knew him to be a boy. Nested in our example is one of the most important challenges facing educators today. Namely, how can we be inclusive of all families and counter opposition when we are being challenged in unprecedented ways, including pushback for such challenges as closing schools for the health and safety of our students and staff, exploring historical injustices, and more? To explore challenges such as these contemporary ones in school districts across the nation, consider the following questions:

1. What steps would you take to ensure that all parents have a voice and that the voices of all parents of color, immigrants, LGBTQ+ parents or kids, etc., are not silenced?
2. Based on your response, how might you explain your reasoning in this hypothetical example?

**Strategies for Understanding and Supporting Identity Safety
in an Inclusive Way**

Consider Sonia's unique reaction to her child's declaration to be identified as a girl:

> Sadly, one of my college students took his life at 24. So, when my daughter came out at 6, I knew the trauma that my student had gone through when he had not been affirmed. [I thought] Okay, I have an opportunity to do things differently. So, I said to my daughter, "All right, baby talk to me, tell me everything, and we'll figure this out.'

> While my husband was very loving, this was earth shattering to him. I'm proud because he was willing to ask, "What steps do I need to follow?" So, we found a gender-affirming child psychologist to help us through this. The psychologist suggested we take our child to the store to choose clothes. When our child tried on a dress, they were so happy and started twirling around.

> My husband's family also struggled at first. However, his mother loved our child unconditionally and showed it. She intuitively understood that she would just love our child as I [and my husband and all of us] figured it out.

                    Reflection Task

Consider Sonia's reaction to her child. How might it influence the reflection response that you initially wrote?

Being inclusive to support every student to reach their potential requires that we be much more accepting, curious about, and welcoming of differences. A good starting point for this purpose is to create a mistake-safe culture where everyone is accepted and supported to be important, contributing, and valuable members. In Chapter 5, we will share ways a school can support the parents/guardians of LGBTQ+ students.

Building a Mistake-Safe Culture

As our schools become increasingly diverse, it is essential to consider operationalizing the positive possibilities of enacting a mistake-safe culture. It gives all members many opportunities to contribute, make mistakes, and receive feedback in a trusting and nonjudgmental way. One way to envision the type of culture we are describing is an interaction we had with a trusted friend about a personal experience that we believe did not go well. As we recount the negative experience, we know that our friend will support us in (1) seeing that we all make mistakes as it is a natural part of the human experience and (2) collaborating in a trusting way to determine the steps that we might take to remedy what happened without undue embarrassment or losing face. In a real sense, our trusted friend is someone we count on because they have our best interest in mind (Zacarian & Silverstone, 2020).

Mistake-safe home-school partnerships involve creating the same type of trust as our example. Its foundation is built on this premise where we know that we can share our ideas, beliefs, and perceptions; hopes and desires; make errors; and receive feedback in ways that have our and the group's best interests in mind (Zacarian & Silverstone, 2020). It is also a culture that works using a strengths-based approach where we help one another to see our individual and collective strengths and believe in the positive possibilities of our working together on behalf of our students. Two key features of a mistake-safe culture:

1. our collectively taking time to examine what is working and what needs strengthening without fear of embarrassment or judgment (Zacarian & Silverstone, 2020); and
2. supporting the momentum of partnerships by crafting mutually agreeable tasks and activities to continually strengthen the partnerships we build.

Here are some general rules for building such home-school partnerships:

- Consistently use a strengths-based approach.
- Be positive and celebrate successes!
- Frame what is going well and what needs strengthening with curiosity.
- View outcomes that are not what is expected as a point for learning and not as failure.
- Support reflection practices throughout.
- Encourage analysis by promoting a positive culture of support. (Zacarian, 2023, p. 177)

The U.S. Department of Education's mission (Gullo et al., 2018) to support all children to reach their full potential calls for us to enact policies and practices that ensure every child's rights are respected. There are many federal laws for this purpose, including the Individuals with Disabilities Act (IDEA) (U.S. Department of Education, n.d.-a) enacted in 1975 and amended in 1990, 1997, and 2004 (Zacarian, 2023), and the Every Student

Succeeds Act (ESSA) enacted in 2011 (U.S. Department of Education, n.d.-b). Despite the intentions of these laws and others to protect the civil rights of students, many actions have been taken to enforce and reinforce their occurrence. One such action is a letter that the U.S. Department of Justice's Civil Rights Division and U.S. Department of Education's Office for Civil Rights sent to every state education agency (SEA) and every public charter school in the nation (U.S. Department of Justice & U.S. Department of Education, January 7, 2015). Why did they send this letter? The Departments of Justice and Education found that many districts across the nation were not following the laws regarding the education of multilingual learners and the rights of their parents. The letter provided guidance about the steps SEAs and districts must take to ensure compliance. In 2020, the U.S. Department of Education reinforced how schools and districts could better ensure the success of their multilingual students (U.S. Department of Education, 2020).

The U.S. Department of Education (2020) supports the formation of "a group of administrators, teachers, counselors, and other staff as well as families and community members to help us evaluate the successes of our language assistance programming and to make changes when needed" (Zacarian, 2023, p. 175). The idea that schools should work together and include family and community members is not novel. What is important is that we rethink how we form such groups to ensure they are as inclusive as possible and reflect the ever-changing population of students and their families.

A more recent example of an initiative to end discrimination is President Biden's proposal to amend Title IX regulations to "strengthen protections for LGBTQ+ students by clarifying that Title IX's protections against discrimination based on sex apply to discrimination based on sexual orientation and gender identity" (U.S Department of Education, 2022, p. 1). President Biden issued a statement on the proposed legislation. In it, he stated:

> I am committed to protecting this progress and working to achieve full equality, inclusion, and dignity for women and girls, LGBTQ+ Americans, all students, and all Americans. My Administration will continue to fight tirelessly to realize the promise of Title IX—that every person deserves an opportunity to pursue their education free from discrimination and realize their full potential. (Biden, 2022)

Biden's executive decision mirrored the 2020 U.S. Supreme Court *Bostock* decision extending antidiscrimination laws to LGBTQ+ workers (National Education Association, 2022). In addition, in June 2021, the U.S. Department of Education's Office for Civil Rights (OCR) issued a Notice of Interpretation entitled "U.S. Department of Education Confirms Title IX Protects Students from Discrimination Based on Sexual Orientation and Gender Identity" (U.S. Department of Education, 2021). The notice of interpretation ensures the rights of students to

- use restrooms or locker rooms that match their affirmed gender identity,
- participate in activities, field trips, and other school events based on their sexual orientation or gender identity, and
- be treated in ways consistent with their gender identity (e.g., correct use of pronouns and names).

(National Education Association, 2022)

While we are being challenged to rethink the laws and regulations to guarantee the rights of the LGBTQ+ community, there is no doubt that we need to work much more collaboratively and inclusively if we are ever to fully support equity amongst all of our diverse students and, most importantly, the identity safety of all students.

SELF-REFLECTION AS A LIFELONG PROCESS

Each of us has a different developmental journey toward identity safety awareness. It is a process that occurs through our unique personal experiences, awareness of the world, and understanding of injustices and how these affect us as well as other individuals and groups of people. For example, we met Vinnie earlier in our book. Vinnie's self-reflective journey began with an awareness of his LGBTQ+ identity at a young age and continued acceptance of his identity at the age of 19. In addition, he is examining his identity as a White male.

It's been an ongoing journey to unpack and unlearn certain things I was exposed to growing up. But luckily, I had the insight to take the time to learn about whiteness and anti-Blackness. I didn't even really know what those terms meant. So, I decided that I needed to learn about what they meant.

I have the privilege to recognize racial inequities, and I can still live a decent life. Meanwhile, people are being harmed while I'm experiencing that privilege, and that's something for all White people, White men in particular. We need to make a concerted effort to learn more about and grapple with whatever emotions come up, whether defensiveness or discomfort. We're not even aware of how our tactics stop the conversation because

of discomfort. What's important for us as individuals is that we calm our
defenses so that we understand and acknowledge that there's a huge difference between impact and intent.

I think it's helpful to be in a space with other White folks, facilitated by an
antiracist expert. So, there's this sense of I can be vulnerable, and I make a
mistake, right? We're going to make mistakes. And to grapple with what I
can learn from this conversation so that I can be a better human being and
we can build a world that's more equitable for individuals, in particular
women and individuals of color, individuals who are religious minorities,
individuals living with a disability, who are not treated the same way that
I'm treated, and not given the same benefits and life that I'm given. It's an
ongoing journey.

HOW WE CAN SHARE VULNERABILITIES

The process of examining our identities is an endeavor that brings us closer
to ourselves and our students. Sometimes the impact is life-changing.

Shining a Light on Revealing Our Vulnerabilities

Daniel, the son of Guatemalan immigrants we met in Chapter 2, shares
an experience with his professor that deeply impacted his life.

I have discovered that the way you build connections with other human beings is by
being vulnerable because you realize that other people are going through the same
emotions as you are. In one of my classes, my Latinx history professor discussed
a book we were reading that touched on some of the sacrifices parents make for
their children. He shared some of his experiences, saying, "I've been a father for a
while, but I realized the sacrifices I've had to make." Right after class, I said, "Hey,
you know, that's interesting when you talked about your family. It got me thinking."
Suddenly I started to cry right in front of my professor; I did not mean to, but it flew
out of me because it made me realize the sacrifices my parents made for me. I told
him that it touched me so deeply.

Then he looked at me crying and asked, "Have you called your parents? Maybe you
should call them."

And I ran out of that classroom, took my bike back to my dorm, and called my mom.
Then I called my grandma. Finally, I called my dad, whom I hadn't talked to in almost

a month. I said, "I may not agree with you on a lot of things, and I do a lot of things you don't approve of, but just know that I love you."

And my dad replied, "Oh, well, I love you too, buddy."

It was the end of the quarter, and I was still in the middle of finals, but I emailed my professor and told him, "I'm never going to forget that moment. Our conversation about parents just meant so much to me."

When I got home for winter break, I continued talking with family members. Having those conversations, I realized it's because they've been hurt or might be coming from a place of hurt. You don't always know what another person is going through. So that's led me to be able to listen to other people outside of my family.

 Reflection Task

1. Describe a time when an interaction supported you in sharing a vulnerability in your life.
2. How did this interaction support or not support your feeling of identity safety?

Often, our students do not tell us about our impact on their lives. Yet, when we take the time to share our vulnerabilities with students, it is an opportunity for students to develop a deeper sense of identity safety (and for us to grow as well!).

PARTNERSHIPS BETWEEN HOME AND SCHOOL

We can help all children grow up to be strong, independent, caring, and nurturing and have a range of life options that previously were earmarked for one gender, race, culture, ethnicity, language group, or another. Sonia demonstrates what is needed in the process of supporting her transgender child. Rather than go it alone, she openly and courageously shares with us the challenges she faced as a parent of a transgender child at home. In Chapter 5, we will learn of Sonia's efforts to support her child's transition at school. Her voice is sorely needed as we evolve to become more inclusive.

One of the most exciting shifts in education is from a hierarchy of leaders at the district and school levels toward a cooperative of working groups composed of administrators, teachers, families, and community members

(Zacarian, 2023). Indeed, we can enact identity safe policies and practices more successfully when we do it together in an inclusive way.

A first step that is important for us as educators is to be open and flexible in building reciprocal and trusted partnerships with and among administrators, teachers, specialists, support staff, and others who make up our school community. A second step is to do the same with the various families in our school. Finally, a third step is doing the same with local community members. Together, we can build on students' pathways to success in ways that might otherwise not have been possible. In Chapter 2, we discussed ways to facilitate Working Groups. An important part of open communication is being able to have honest conversations about race and gender.

FACILITATING CONVERSATIONS ABOUT MULTIDIVERSE IDENTITIES

Holding respectful dialogue to learn about each other's perspectives is another challenging but powerful way to support identity safety. It gives everyone a voice, builds bridges of empathy across the community, and helps parents/guardians support their children. These conversations are best if held before a problem or incident occurs, although it does not guarantee they will never occur. Whenever a racist, homophobic, or transphobic incident happens, these conversations are crucial to initiating healing. We recommend some tips for facilitating these conversations.

- Communicate the goals of the meeting and follow a clear, focused agenda.
- Use "Community Agreements" to ensure civility while allowing people to speak their truth without blaming or attacking. Here are some examples:
  » Give everyone a chance to speak and avoid interrupting.
  » Use "I" statements and speak for ourselves only.
  » Do not try to represent a whole group or ask others to do so.
  » Hang in through the hard moments, even with truths that are hard to hear.
  » Value confidentiality so people can freely share feelings and stories. (adapted from Not In Our Town https://www.niot.org /nios/implementingnios#6)
- Encourage participants to speak up if they hear a microaggression or when something that has been said causes discomfort. Allow space for the participant who was insensitive to apologize and commit to not doing it again.

- Remind the group of the agreements if a conflict emerges. Ask participants to listen and consider different perspectives. Then, guide them to see the values they have in common.
- Inform members that sometimes meetings will end without closure. If that occurs, summarize key points at the end and return to the topic later.

LOOKING AHEAD

In this chapter, we explored the importance of self-reflection for examining our own identities and implicit and explicit biases to support identity safe spaces. We also presented steps that we can take to build reflective home-school partnerships. In the next chapter, we will examine how people develop their identities. We will consider positive and negative experiences that deeply influence a person's identity to understand better how to support identity safety.

ADDITIONAL RESOURCES

- **Supporting Positive Habits of Mind**
  Costa, A. L., & Kallick, B. (2018). *Habits of mind: Strategies for disciplined choice making*. Systems Thinking. https://thesystemsthinker.com/habits-of-mind-strategies-for-disciplined-choice-making/
- **Student Self-Reflection**
  Zacarian, D., & Silverstone, M. A. (2020). Student self-reflection. In *Teaching to empower: Taking action to foster student agency, self-confidence, and collaboration* (pp. 82–100). ASCD.
- **Teacher Self-Assessment**
  Cohn-Vargas, B., Kahn, A. C., Epstein, A., & Gogolewski, K. (2022). *Belonging and inclusion in identity safe schools: A guide for educational leaders* (Appendix B). Corwin.

CHAPTER 4

Supporting Positive Identity Development

Aurora Haynes is a university professor in a graduate program and her husband, Ray, is a school principal. They apply identity safe practices at home with their children, ages 2 and 4.

> Both my husband and I are Black biracial people. We try to help our sons feel free to be authentic. We want them to feel openness, curiosity, and flexibility to not adhere to racialized norms, cultural norms, or gender norms. We want them to be caring, compassionate, and kind and value family. We have the opportunity to help our sons understand and learn how to navigate the world.

A positive identity emerges as a child feels a sense of dignity and self-worth and learns to relate to others in the world around them. As we discovered in previous chapters, parents/guardians and educators communicate the power of their unique identity in ways that draw on their personal and cultural assets. We can help children to find their voice, feel seen and heard, and acknowledge their many social identities (e.g., athlete, good conversationalist, collaborator, artist, musician, etc.). Different identities are salient, meaning they stand out and are essential to us at different times and in different contexts. For example, one of us, Becki, has a 2-year-old grandson, Anteo. Anteo names a variety of dinosaur species as he views picture books on the topic. He is also becoming increasingly aware of the insects he sees. His parents and Becki continuously reward his curiosity about and recollections of the names of the dinosaurs and insects with affirmations of how amazing he is at remembering facts and how they see his emerging identity as a biologist. Perhaps, these types of interactions are familiar to you. Indeed, children have a range of interactions that support their confidence. However, they also experience communication that can lead to feelings of insecurity and shame. We all want to support children to develop the skills needed to resist direct and indirect influences that undermine the formation of positive identities, including stereotyping, microaggressions, and bullying.

In this chapter, we explore the following:

- Supporting positive identity development at home and school
- Helping children to counter negative influences that undermine positive identity formation
- Building and strengthening home-school partnerships that support children's identities

WHAT IS POSITIVE IDENTITY DEVELOPMENT, AND WHY DOES IT MATTER?

Positive identity development refers to experiences leading to a child's feelings of dignity and self-worth. An example is Jesús, whom we met in Chapter 3. Despite attending a school that prohibited speaking Spanish and did not expect more than a few Latinx students to graduate, let alone attend college, Jesús recounts the influence of his sole Chicano teacher.

> When I finished high school, I was scared about going to college. I chose to major in chemistry. Why? Because my only Chicano teacher, Mr. Pérez, was a chemistry teacher. Since I have a great memory and can rattle off the periodic table without missing a beat, I decided to become a chemist, never knowing what the hell that meant. I graduated as a chemistry major.

Mr. Pérez was a role model for Jesús. He influenced Jesús's career as a chemist and the confidence to find his true calling. Later, Jesús became a journalist and the Director of Communications and Public Affairs at the Harvard University Kennedy School of Government. Currently, Jesús is finishing a historical novel entitled *Blood at the Roots* that takes place on the Texas-Mexico border where he was reared.

Three of the crucial goals of supporting children's positive identity development include:

1. giving children many positive experiences to affirm their multiple and varied identities;
2. strengthening their ever-growing awareness; and
3. helping them to build the tools needed to deconstruct, dismantle, and counteract the power of negative experiences that undermine a sense of identity.

Identity in the Context of Child Development

Healthy child development, introduced in Chapter 2, integrates physical, cognitive, sexual, emotional, social, and spiritual growth with the ever-presence of social interactions. Interactions that support a child's sense of safety, belonging, self-worth, and competence set the stage for connecting to the outside world. With our schema of supporting positive interactions and lots of them, we aim to build a repository to counterbalance negative messages and experiences.

Identity as a Learner

When we use student-centered teaching practices, we support students to develop a robust academic identity that they are smart, capable learners who can experience school success. The SISP study researched specific components that strengthened a child's academic identity (Cohn-Vargas et al., 2021; Steele, 2012):

- *Listening for student voices* that promotes confidence as students contribute to classroom life.
- *Teaching for understanding* to ensure students gain competence, knowledge, and skills.
- *Cultivating diversity as a resource for learning* to help children experience their multidiverse identities as assets.

According to the SISP study, students who felt identity safe engaged in rigorous academic studies, trusted their intelligence and capacity for success, and became motivated as learners.

Reflection Task

1. What experiences contributed to your academic identity and sense of competence?
2. How do you strengthen your students' identity as learners?

Here are some ways to instill competence in a child:

At home and school:

- ensure children comprehend what they are learning and reading by asking critical-thinking questions;

- use culturally responsive practices that draw upon a child's prior knowledge providing tasks that build academic skills;
- promote curiosity and validate taking risks to try new things; and
- turn errors, mistakes, and failures into learning opportunities.

Multidiverse Identity Development

Although race is a social and not a biological construct, racial categories are ever-present in society (Lewis, 2003). Racial stereotypes cause people to be treated as if their identities are fixed and significantly impact children from a young age (Lewis, 2003; Tatum, 1997). Seminal researcher Jean Phinney (1990) studied identity development in African Americans, Latinx, and Asian-Pacific Islanders. Her research describes three stages of racial/ethnic identity development and can be applied across identities. Helpful ways for enacting these stages with multidiverse students at home and school are presented in our next section.

Three Stages of Ethnic Identity Development (Phinney, 1990)

Stage 1: Unexamined Identity

> Children, and in some cases, teens and adults who have not yet explored their identity, generally absorb the messages and attitudes experienced at home, in their community, and in the larger world around them, often without questioning. (Phinney, 1990)

At home and school:

- offer numerous positive messages through dialogue, role models, books, and films that validate a child's background;
- verbally articulate validation of many social identities without resorting to stereotypes;
- talk about differences in identity in ways that embrace the rich diversity of all people;
- limit access to people and media messages that demean a child's race, language, ethnicity, religion, gender, and other diverse identities;
- help reduce the impact of potentially harmful influences. For example, when a child experiences a microaggression or encounters a racial/ethnic/linguistic/religious slur, talk about it, and help children understand that it is wrong and unfair; and
- stop children from teasing or bullying others.

Stage 2: Identity Search

Youth, as they mature, and some adults begin a period of exploration by trying to understand the significance and meaning of their racial/ethnic and other multidiverse identities (Phinney, 1990).

At home and school:

- encourage children to explore their identities without judgment or defining their identities for them;
- provide opportunities to meet and spend time with people who share their identities and form affinity groups;
- help them develop openness to diverse identities and an antiracist stance; and
- help process feelings that emerge as they encounter negative or demeaning messages in their world or the greater society.

Stage 3: Identity Achievement

During this stage, a person accepts and internalizes a sense of racial/ethnic identity (Phinney, 1990).

At home and school:

- validate children in the process of reaching identity achievement; and
- continue to connect with people who share their identities and introduce role models who share their backgrounds. Provide opportunities to connect with people from different backgrounds.

While there is limited research on White identity development, researchers know that young children experience the power dynamics that benefit the larger White society (Derman-Sparks & Ramsey, 2006). As a result, they inevitably start learning, developing, and performing the meanings associated with White-identity roles (Van Ausdale & Feagan, 2001). Author Gary Howard writes about privilege, power, and the role of White leaders and educators in a multicultural society. In *We Can't Teach What We Don't Know: White Teachers, Multiracial Schools* (1999), he declares that "most of the early work exploring White racial identity formation was related to the issue of racism and learning to acknowledge and overcome this through developing a more inclusive anti-racist sense of White identity" (p. 88). Antiracist scholar Ibram X. Kendi (2019) defines an antiracist as a person from any racial group who believes that all racial groups are equal and works to reduce racial inequity (p. 25). Kendi's contributions offer new insights on how parents/guardians and educators can play a crucial part at all stages of children's development by better ensuring an abundance of (1) positive interactions, (2) countering negative interactions, and (3) everyone's role in addressing and redressing systemic racism.

 Reflection Task

Reflect on your earliest awareness of your racial/ethnic identity.

1. How did your racial, cultural, linguistic, and ethnic identity emerge and change over time?
2. How do you support identity development in multidiverse students?
3. What more can you do?

Gender Identity and Sexual Orientation Development

By age 2, children notice physical differences between boys and girls; by age 4 (according to the American Academy of Pediatrics), "most children have a stable sense of their gender identity" (Gender Spectrum, n.d.). However, not all people discover their gender identity at the same developmental stage. The term cisgender describes people who identify with the gender they were assigned at birth. It is important to note that some cisgender children prefer nonstereotypical clothing or toys (e.g., cars, dolls, etc.). Meanwhile, others identify as transgender, nonbinary, or anywhere along a spectrum between male and female, including some whose identities are fluid. Gender develops separately from sexual orientation, which refers to whom a person is attracted to in a physical, emotional, or romantic way.

In the TEDWomen Talk *The Way We Think About Biological Sex Is Wrong*, Emily Quinn (2018) explains that gender identity is influenced by more than what is viewed on the outside. Besides genitalia, it includes other factors: hormones, chromosomes, and secondary sex characteristics (hair and breast development). Quinn shares that she was born with XY chromosomes, known as male chromosomes, and both male and female sex organs. She states that intersex individuals make up approximately 2% of the population, which is equal to the population of red-headed people. Adults can validate a range of gender expressions and refrain from labeling a child. We can also offer children the freedom to explore their gender identities while communicating positive attitudes about people across the gender spectrum. In identity safety, we aim to allow children to be themselves in ways that break out of gender binaries. We want children to freely express themselves and experience the world without having gender stereotypes that limit the possibilities for fulfillment as human beings.

Reflection Task

Reflect on your gender identity and sexuality.

1. Describe one or more gender identity experience(s) from your childhood.
2. How have these influenced your beliefs about gender now?
3. What can you do at work to ensure that your school or community is identity safe for students, staff, and families of all gender identities?

Language, Culture, and Family History Development

The people we interviewed for this book shared countless examples of their families' home languages, traditions, and cultures through family stories and ways of communicating and acting. These included stories about food and preparing meals, dance, and storytelling, as well as about using a language other than English to communicate with a loved one. All of these are tied or in addition to their unique experiences and identities. In the following examples, Pooja, the environmental activist we met in Chapter 1, shares that the Gujarati language is integral to her identity. Also, Latinx school principal Isacc, who is bilingual and bicultural, makes an effort to affirm students' and families' home languages.

Shining a Light on Valuing Multilingual Identities

Environmental activisit Pooja says

Many people in my generation cannot speak our language or speak broken Gujarati. I was lucky; every Wednesday, I attended a free Gujarati class where I learned to read and write my language. Meanwhile, at home, I practiced speaking it with my family.

Principal Isacc tries to learn a few words in each language so that he may acknowledge the various representatives in his school.

I welcome them by saying the following in their home language, "Good morning. My name is Mr. Villanueva."

He also takes time to listen to families and support them in sharing the gifts of their primary languages with their children. One of Isacc's important identities and one that he tries to engender with students and families is the high value of a student's home language and the connection it has to the language and cultural

traditions that have been passed down through generations. As you read what
Isacc shares with us, consider the high value he places on language and culture.

"Please don't stop speaking your language at home. Your children need to speak
their language. It's an aspect of your family, . . . if you don't, you start losing connections to ancestors and relatives who [are the only ones who] speak that language.
It's also so important for us to be bilingual."

One of the most essential aspects of multidiverse identity is the connection between language and culture. Anthropologist Michael Agar (1995,
2006) coined the term "languaculture" to mean the indelible tie between
language and culture. School principal Isacc brings this idea to the forefront
of his work with students and their families. He sees the essential value of
home languages and cultures in supporting students' identity safety.

Affirming Our Names, Traditions, and Stories

Our names often reflect our family history and strengthen connections to
our various cultures, traditions, and identities. One of us, Becki, gave her
children Spanish names that link to the Nicaraguan part of their identity.
The other member of our author team, Debbie, gave her children names
that are linked to her and her husband's ancestry. Identity safe educators
aim to pronounce children's names and honor name changes correctly.
They also teach students never to bully a child about their name.

Around the dinner table, amidst the flavors of unique foods, many family
stories are shared. For example, Becki's husband prepares Nicaraguan food and
shares stories from his childhood in Managua using Spanish, his home language. Another example is Chen, a program manager for extended learning at
the Oakland Unified School District. While her husband is a White American,
Chen was reared in Cambodia and came to the United States as a young
Cambodian refugee. In their home, dinner time is filled with stories about
Chen's immigrant experiences amidst foods that represent her Cambodian
culture as well as her husband's experiences. Their conversations help support
their child's multicultural, multiracial, and multiethnic background.

Evelyn loves Cambodian food. Yesterday, we had green curry chicken. I
told her how I would help my mom prepare food for our entire family of
eight. Given my parents' journey from Cambodia to the U.S., they wouldn't
talk about the past. Silence was an unspoken rule so, staying silent was my
way of being obedient while chopping vegetables and preparing rice. Now,
with my daughter, as we are preparing the curry or making egg rolls, we

not only talk about ingredients but share my family history. One example that I shared with her was that growing up, we often did not have enough money to buy food to feed everyone in the family. I told her that when I was 12 and living in Modesto, my mom would stand in line to get huge blocks of American cheese and canned processed pork and then not know how to use it to make Cambodian food.

Chen and her husband infuse conversations such as this one to help Evelyn understand her parents' different lived experiences. Their evening meal supports them in having meaningful conversations about their multicultural life experiences.

At school, educators can make space for students to bring their traditions forward in different ways, including sharing family stories, reading literature, and engaging in discussions and projects across the curriculum. For example, Paula, the Menominee educator we met earlier, shares a story about a gym teacher at the Indian Community School where she worked. "For every sport this teacher introduces, from basketball to football and others, she teaches the Indigenous game it originated from that preceded it" (Cohn-Vargas & Rabideaux, 2023, p. 43).

TAKING ACTION

Identity safe spaces promote healthy identity development, offering opportunities to practice skills, counteract negative influences, and form positive relationships with peers and adults. Parents/guardians are the first and most significant contributors to children's pride in their backgrounds and identities. They instill values and can give children a solid foundation in the positive qualities of their backgrounds and the many social identities they possess. Educators can reinforce positive identity development by encouraging children to express themselves authentically. Schools can reinforce home and community traditions by exploring family stories and learning about a family's personal, social, academic, and linguistic cultures and more. In the SISP domain, *Cultivating Diversity as a Resource for Teaching* highlighted the importance of drawing from a child's multidiverse background as part of the school curriculum (Steele, 2012).

Validating a Child's Identity Through Listening and Caring

We want to empower students to have a sense of agency. Supporting empowerment occurs when we listen to students' interactions and affirm and acknowledge what they share by demonstrating our sense of caring about and for them through what we say (Zacarian and Silverstone, 2020).

**Shining a Light on Relationships That Validate
Student Identities**

The following example illustrates the type of interaction that supported Paula's
daughter's Menominee identity.

> One day, a teacher asked, "I heard you have a Powwow on your reservation this
> weekend. Are you going?" My daughter looked at her, amazed; no one had ever
> asked her about anything Indigenous.
>
> "Yeah, there is," she replied.
>
> The teacher continued, "If you go, maybe you can tell me about it next week."
>
> It made her day, giving her an uplifting feeling that the teacher cared. From then on,
> my daughter loved this teacher and got an A in her course. To this day, she's her fa-
> vorite teacher. With Native students, there is no secret to culturally responsive prac-
> tices; the main ingredient is relationship. (Cohn-Vargas & Rabideaux, 2023, p. 41)

Relationships can be built through simple acts of validation and offering
space for making lifelong contributions to a positive identity. It is helpful
for children, especially in situations where they are the minority, to be with
people who share their background. As lesbian parents, Judy and Allison
felt their children needed to experience environments where they were
not always the only children with same-sex parents. Judy organized gatherings for gay and lesbian families:

> When our children were young, I started organizing a group family hostel
> experience in the summer. Eventually, we started going twice a year. We
> continue doing it even as our kids are now in and done with college. Our
> son, Kobi, and his best friend are the oldest; they are both 25. The younger
> generation is all super close, almost like cousins.

Reflection Task

Reflect on family stories and traditions.

1. How do you invite students and families to share their language, cultural,
   and home traditions?
2. How can you enrich the experience by inviting students' families and
   communities into the classroom?

Cultivating a Positive Gender Identity

Having a positive gender identity is vital for every child along the gender spectrum. Adults can offer options for children to express themselves freely, modeling and discussing alternatives to gender stereotypes. For example, Carlee, a trauma-responsive educator, a former high school teacher, and mother of two shares,

> My husband and I identify as White, cisgender, and straight. We want our children to explore gender without stereotypes or limitations. We read books about the gender spectrum. Four-year-old Frankie and one-year-old Aleya have many dress-up clothes to try on and baby dolls for everybody. Frankie feels comfortable asking, "Is it okay if I feel like a girl today?"
>
> And I reply, "Of course." I don't know why he even is still asking.

Another example is Sameer, a college freshman whose immigrant parents from India and Pakistan let him play freely.

> At 4, I told my parents I wanted to be a girl. They asked, "Do you want to change to be a girl?" I replied, "No, but I wish I were born a girl." I told them I wanted to play with dolls and wear dresses. They let me have lots of dolls and dress as Cinderella for Halloween with clip-on earrings, glass slippers, and a dress, and they even painted my nails. I liked that and felt comfortable.

We can help children become strong, independent, caring, and nurturing in ways that were once stereotyped as a specific gender. We can make identity safe spaces for children of all gender identities and sexual orientations.

Supporting Children With Multiple Heritages

According to the U.S. Census, the multiracial population jumped from 9 million in 2010 to 33.8 million in 2020 (Jones et al., 2021). Having multiple racial or religious identities offers a rich mixture of backgrounds but can also present various challenges. As Aurora described at the start of this chapter, children with mixed identities often navigate their identities in unique ways. Sameer explains how he navigated two ethnicities and religions.

> I am half Indian Hindu and half Pakistani Muslim. I grew up reading Indian comic books that tell the mythology. I also grew up with a Quran for kids. However, both sides of my family have never met each other. So, when

the Muslim side of the family would visit, we'd take down the painting of Ganesh, the elephant-headed Hindu god. And when the Hindu side came over, we'd remove the Arabic calligraphy from the wall. Both sides of my family wanted me to define my religious identity and pick a side. I didn't want to, so I didn't. Luckily, my parents worked to instill pride in both aspects of my culture and encouraged me not to feel I had to pick a side.

Some people with multiracial ancestry face assumptions about their identity because of their skin color. Aurora, whom we met at the beginning of this chapter, describes what she and her husband, Ray, experienced:

Growing up mixed race, Ray and I have had to navigate belonging and create our own spaces. Unfortunately, the notion of Blackness in the United States is defined very narrowly. Frequently, societal forces about Blackness, social class, and other things can fracture or impact relationships.

Aurora points out that the diversity of the Black community includes Caribbean, Latinx American, African people, and more.

Having an awareness of the many representations of Blackness expands what it means to be able to be who you are, contributing to a positive sense of identity. It's a gift that our extended family includes Blacks, Whites, and Latinos with largely mixed-race children. In addition, our family includes several religions, Judaism, Christianity, and Islam. By virtue of my family, we have these kinds of conversations and exposure to different people. It makes the idea of fitting into some stereotypical category to achieve membership untrue.

Some people with mixed heritages perceive that they are only partially accepted by people of either background. In other cases, they feel they do not belong to either background. For example, Nicole, the student teacher we met in Chapter 1, has a Japanese mother and a White father. Nicole dislikes being asked to check off a box to describe her identity, saying, "If I mark White, it feels like I'm ignoring an enormous part of my identity. However, if I mark both, it feels like I'm trying to claim something or join a club I am not a part of."

Randi grew up feeling different with her blonde hair and the Asian features inherited from her Japanese grandmother. Her life changed after being photographed for a book by Kip Fulbeck, entitled *Part Asian, 100% Hapa* (2006). In Hawaii, Hapa is a term used to describe people who are partially Asian or Pacific Islander. Kip, mixed Chinese and Irish himself, photographed an array of beautiful portraits of Hapa people. The message is clear; nobody is "half" anything, which is a powerful message to people of mixed ancestry. Randi explains that the experience made a huge difference in her life. She no longer feels she must explain her identity to anyone. She is proud to be Hapa.

Aurora sums up the way she and her husband, Ray, are raising their sons, saying,

> By the time our kids, James and Alexander, have grown up we hope they will have learned that race in and of itself is a social construct that is problematic. That said we aim for them to have a deep pride in their Blackness and membership in the Black Diaspora and they have the freedom to define their own identities and make sense of what is of most meaning to themselves.

At home and school:

- communicate the value of diversity and the benefits of all identities, including mixed backgrounds, without singling children out;
- share the concept that nobody is "half" or "part" of an ethnicity; and
- ensure that children of mixed backgrounds are not excluded or bullied and find ways to address it. This happens through taking time to observe and notice.

Countering the Impact of Racial Trauma, Homophobia, Transphobia, and Other Forms of Bias

Given the prevalence of bias in society, we must seek effective ways to help children navigate the challenges and negative influences in their immediate environment and the larger world. Cultural misunderstandings, stereotypes, microaggressions, and discrimination can—and all too often, do—harm a child's sense of identity safety and diminish their sense of self-worth. In Chapter 1, we discussed othering and saw evidence of negative stereotyping in the form of stereotype threat that lowers academic performance. In Chapter 3, we introduced Hardy's depictions of racial trauma. Here we describe how racial trauma manifests. For example, *internalized devaluation* resounds in the person's head and signals, "I am unworthy; I am a bad person; I cannot achieve."

Hardy (2013) describes an *assaulted sense of self* resulting from myriad negative messages and assumptions. Lisha, the physician we met in Chapter 1, shares two powerful experiences exemplifying Hardy's significant contribution.

My friend and I were 20-year-old college students. One cold day, we were in a department store wearing winter jackets. Suddenly, the manager called security because he thought we were stealing. I am thinking, "Hey, my parents work hard; my dad is paying thousands of dollars for me to attend this school; we don't need to steal anything." The security guards made us take our jackets off. They looked in our pockets because they were sure we had stolen something. Nevertheless, of course, they found nothing.

Recently, I was reminded of the burden I carry every single day. I had traveled to Spain with my daughter, Acacia. We were in a little boutique with perfume, purses, rings, and cute things you want to touch and pick up. I immediately told Acacia, 'Don't pick anything up; Don't touch anything; don't try on any rings. Keep your hands where they can be seen." Soon, I realized these people weren't watching us. They didn't think we were going to steal anything. Suddenly, a weight lifted off my shoulders. Unfortunately, this is what I endure at home in the U.S., what I live with all the time. Ever since I hit puberty, I have been surveilled and followed in stores.

The harm caused by Hardy's delineation of racial trauma is also caused by homophobia, transphobia, and many other forms of discrimination. Sameer, for example, was relentlessly bullied for his perceived gender expression and for acting "like a girl." He grew up among fellow South Asians, where being gay was never discussed. Then, the bullying became explicitly homophobic. He would hear "you're so gay" frequently from 5th- to 8th-grade peers even though he didn't know what the term gay meant. He did not report it because it often happened in front of teachers who never intervened. His peers' actions and his teachers' inactions made him worried that maybe he deserved it, saying, "I felt ashamed."

You might ask, what can schools do to counteract humiliating and hurtful experiences? The answer is that there is a lot we can and must do! Sameer offers a fine example of the difference he experienced when he transferred to a different school.

My new school was great for me. On the first day, I met the other first-year students. One stood up and said, "Hey, by the way, I use they-them pronouns." I'd never heard of that and went home to google it. What struck me was that I'd been bullied and taught that being gay is something to avoid at all costs, yet here, people were proud to call themselves gay. I lay awake at night, thinking about my identity, and eventually came to terms with it. Joining a GSA (Gender-Sexuality Alliance) club, I learned other people's stories and didn't feel so alone.

I was the first person to come out in our South Asian community. At 14, I came out to my parents. I helped bring them around by sharing the statistics and information I learned at school. They always promised they'd love me no matter what, but when they understood what this meant to me, they were 100% supportive and decided to post on Facebook. They made it clear that anyone who didn't support me wouldn't be part of our life anymore. It was incredibly courageous of them and, obviously, the right thing to do.

Instilling Joy in Students

Lenore teaches in a community college program called Umoja, from the Kiswahili word meaning unity (https://umojacommunity.org). The program focuses on teaching English composition and counseling services through an African diasporic lens. and enhancing the cultural and educational experiences of students of African descent as a foundation for academic success.

Shining a Light on the Power of Joy

Lenore explains how she designed her program and what happened when she did.

I decided that instead of only talking about the tragedies and injustices of history, which I know are important to talk about, I wanted to make it about Black joy. I want students to be proud to be Black, feel pride in their identity, and talk about things that edify our souls. So, I named the class "Soul Food Recipes for Black Joy." We literally learned about soul food, but also studied Black literature and music and ended the course with Black humor.

One assignment was to talk about the role of African American Vernacular English (AAVE) in the Black community. The students were assigned an essay weighing the pros and cons of AAVE. Two groups of young women got into an impassioned argument about whether Black folks should be using AAVE at all. I was thrilled that there was so much investment in the argument. Some young women suggested that people should stop using it because it wouldn't help them get ahead in the world. Other young women felt that it's part of our culture and our past, and it's essential to keep us grounded in the rich history of our language. Several days later, the students were working on their essays with them. One young lady was sitting there, not doing anything. Then she said, "I'm really sorry. I'm just so overwhelmed with emotion right now because I've never had an opportunity to talk about something so important to me in an English class where I felt what I was talking about really mattered."

It moved me that my student felt this way. So often, especially people on the right, critique this idea of representation. However, they don't really know how soul-satisfying it is when somebody recognizes that your culture matters, that the place where you come from matters and that the people you come from matter. It's not just a nice way to build self-esteem; there is an intellectual weight, a cultural weight. There are ramifications if I am using Ebonics in a situation where I recognize all of the nuances of communication, how I'm being perceived by one audience, and how another is perceiving me. When someone gives voice to it, it is so powerful.

By the time they submitted their essays, the young women who had decided that AAVE had no value changed their minds, not wholly, but they had modified their view with a more nuanced understanding because of that conversation with their peers. It wasn't something that I said. It was them having that conversation, that dynamic, that intersection of passionate discussion. That is what you go to college for, to be engaged on that level. I was so happy that I was able to facilitate some experience like that for them.

Reflection Task

1. Name 2–3 aspects of Lenore's Umoja course that foster identity safety.
2. How do you incorporate these aspects in your teaching, or how might you include them in the future?

While we cannot stop all negative encounters, we can inoculate children against inevitable negativity and biases with numerous positive identity experiences. Scholar Sonia Nieto (1998, 1999) claims that positive actions such as these can and do value students' backgrounds, develop solidarity across differences, and foster the capacity to rectify systemic barriers and inequities. We believe that the opportunity for students to truly embrace, celebrate, and be joyful about their multidiverse identities is critical for identity safety.

At home and school:

- instill pride, embrace diversity, and validate children's authentic selves;
- teach the truth about history and efforts to abolish slavery, fight for civil and human rights, and gender equity;
- help children understand the historical roots of bias and how it plays out in the present. Help them critically analyze any of their negative or biased experiences, lessening the impact;

- immediately address microaggressions, bullying, and other biased behaviors in ways that educate rather than punish;
- incorporate "food for the soul" that inspires children to feel joy and celebrate their rich assets coming from their families, cultures, and the indomitable human spirit; and
- teach them to be upstanders who speak up for themselves and others. (We will discuss this further in Chapter 5.)

Intersectionality: Supporting Students With Multiple Social Identities

Law professor Kimberlé Crenshaw (2020) coined the term "intersectionality" to describe a person who has more than one marginalized identity, saying, "if you're standing in the path of multiple forms of exclusion, you're likely to get hit by both." For example, a transgender person of color will likely encounter oppression or discrimination for both identities. They may meet White transgender people with biases against people of color. Also, they may be subject to stereotypes about transgender people by others who share their racial identity. When different aspects of identity are subject to unequal status, students suffer another form of an" assaulted sense of self."

Isacc, the principal we met earlier, discussed his challenges as a parent. He is Latinx, his husband is White, and they have three children. Their two boys are blond and blue-eyed, and their daughter has dark skin and dark hair and is Mexican and Chinese. Isacc described what he and his husband have had to learn from each other.

> I had to be honest and tell my husband that I don't know how to raise a White boy, and we discussed the kind of privilege our sons have compared to our daughter. In the past, I have had frustrating conversations with my mom and other family members about how they talk about the kids and compare my daughter to her cousin, who has light skin, and who everyone says is so cute. I had to explain to my husband about the ingrained colorism and internalized racism. I told him that would be prevalent in many White-appearing families, and we need you to protect her. I need you to help her celebrate her identity and appearance, as well as help her learn to stand up for herself.

Educators can support students and their families by

1. examining our biases. For example, some parents/guardians represent the same racial, cultural, linguistic, and ethnic heritage as ours, whereas others do not. Are we more comfortable with the

parents/guardians who share our backgrounds? What steps must
we take to support us in being more curious, open, and caring to
all family members?;

2. learning about intersectionality and noticing how oppression and
discrimination manifest in situations;

3. acknowledging, validating, and honoring students' intersectional
identities;

4. helping students speak up if they are experiencing exclusion or
bias for any aspect of their identity;

5. immediately responding to bullying, bias, exclusion, and name-
calling within and between groups while simultaneously
supporting, valuing, and affirming students' various identities; and

6. engaging in an open dialogue with staff, students, and families to
raise awareness, support intersectionality, and stop people from
making value judgments, including comparing who has suffered
more.

Identity Safety Cues (ISCs)

School environments have cues and unspoken messages that either signal
"you belong here" or the reverse, "you don't belong here" (Purdie-Vaughns
et al., 2008). For example, how would you feel as a Black student attending a school named after Robert E. Lee? How would you feel if you are a
student from El Salvador researching current events and find an article describing Central American immigrants as thieves and drug dealers? Each of
these examples should raise awareness about the important findings from
stereotype threat research. The research demonstrated that when people
feel they are being judged by a negative stereotype, their performance
drops (Steele, 2011).

Conversely, researchers have shown the effectiveness of identity safety
cues [ISCs] for all students, including those from stigmatized *and* nonstig-
matized groups (Howansky et al., 2021). For example, in one ISC study,
a professor developed a syllabus with a nondiscrimination policy that included three ISC cues of (1) a rainbow; (2) a "this is adversity-safe space"
graphic; and (3) the instructor's preferred pronouns accompanied with a
hyperlink to learn about pronouns. The control group had the same syllabus without these three ISCs. Results showed that "participants in the class
with the ISCs in the syllabus believed their professor was trying to create a
more inclusive classroom and disapproved of social inequalities more than
participants in the control course [and] . . . reported a higher sense of belonging and fewer absences" (Howansky et al., 2021, p. 1).

Reflection Task

Reflect on ISCs.

1. What environmental cues are present in your classroom (e.g., posters, slides, literature, rainbow flags, photos representing multidiverse people)?
2. How do you model and signal inclusion with your words and actions?
3. How do you include diverse perspectives in your curriculum and provide opportunities for students to see people like themselves?

PARTNERSHIPS BETWEEN HOME AND SCHOOL

Partnering with families offers invaluable opportunities to learn from and with each other, share resources, and support positive student identity development. For example, one of us (Debbie) worked with an elementary school of dominant English speakers and South and Central American and Caribbean students who were in its language education program. We created a school play delivered entirely in Spanish. English- and Spanish-speaking students tried out for the play, and all were selected! Latinx parents, who had not previously been involved in their child's school, volunteered to make costumes, and provided refreshments. Many American English-fluent parents joined their efforts. The play was wildly successful and showcased the possibilities that can happen when we genuinely create welcoming partnerships.

Fostering Parent/Guardian Identity Safety

When discussing an identity safe home-school partnership, we must seek ways to consider and support parent/guardian identity safety intentionally. It serves to validate, include, and honor parents and guardians for who they are and the tremendous love and care they give their children and sends a positive message to their children of the value, respect, and care we hold for them.

Listen to Parents/Guardians to Help Build Home-School Connections

Just as we must be open, curious, and nonjudgmental with our students, we must be the same with parents and guardians. It can be harmful to do otherwise, despite our best intentions. We can build connections on behalf of children's school success. The following is another example from Paula, the Menominee parent and educator. She shares her recollection of her son's interaction with his teacher.

Shining a Light on Interdependence

As you read the example, consider Paula's actions to support her son.

When my son's progress report had a low participation grade, I asked him, "What happened?"

He answered, "A group of boys always talks during class, and I couldn't concentrate, so I sat on the opposite side of the room to focus."

So, I contacted the teacher to help him appreciate our culture and recognize that my son's behaviors were not uninvolved but rather his way of learning. I told the teacher, "Currently, my son doesn't have a relationship with you. Once you develop a relationship, he'll feel more comfortable looking at you and participating. Please find things you have in common with him. Then, take him aside quietly, being careful not to do it in front of the class. Ask how it's going or if he needs help. Once a relationship grows, you can high-five him. Until then, it's uncomfortable for him."

Then I told my son, "Your teacher isn't used to your behaviors as a Native boy. Try sometimes looking up and nodding. It's how the dominant culture interacts; you'll feel more comfortable making eye contact as you develop a relationship."

After I met with my son's teacher for half an hour, he told me, "I've learned more from you about Native students [today] than I have in the twenty years I've been teaching here."

Eventually, my son and his teacher connected, and my son did very well in his class. (Cohn-Vargas & Rabideaux, 2023, p. 41)

As educators, we know the importance of being aware of the impact of our actions, but even the most seasoned of us may inadvertently be insensitive. However, when someone points it out, as the open and curious educators we aspire to be, we can listen, apologize, be accountable, and work to rectify the situation.

Reflection Task

Have you ever had an experience where a parent or student was upset with how you handled a situation?

1. How did you respond?
2. How might you respond differently today?

Developmentally Appropriate Conversations About Differences

Children from pre-K–12 benefit from conversations that teach them about multidiverse identities (Cohn-Vargas et al., 2022; Zacarian & Silverstone, 2020; Zacarian & Soto, 2020). We can have conversations at school and encourage parents/guardians to have conversations at home.

We can teach children about the unique and special qualities that each of us possesses. We can demonstrate how to treat others with kindness and fairness in our words and actions so that children experience models of positive interactions with multidiverse people. Many tools demonstrate multidiversity, including crayons of different skin tones and books for all age groups depicting multidiverse characters and people enacting positive roles. Equally important are resources that support children in being collaborative and engaging in self-advocacy by listening to others, expressing empathy, paying attention to others' values, assets and strengths, mediating emotions, and resolving conflict productively (Zacarian & Silverstone, 2020, p. 17).

As children grow older, they become increasingly aware of injustice. This is particularly true for students living in diverse communities where the populace experiences racism, bias, stereotyping, and more. Young children can learn the meaning of these phenomena in simple and age-appropriate terms. They can also learn that everyone makes mistakes, acknowledges these, and continues to mature. As they mature and become more aware of current events, encourage them to ask questions, share feelings, and learn to

- speak up if someone is harmed and stand up to unfair or unjust treatment;
- counter negative stereotypes, mean comments, and racist attitudes in simple language; and
- self-advocate.

In middle and high school, students also can explore and share their own identities at a deeper level. Through ongoing conversations, listen to their feelings and help them:

- explore and share their own identity with pride;
- learn about racism, homophobia, and other forms of prejudice and discuss controversial topics respectfully; and
- take a proactive stand against all forms of injustice and bias.

Positively Countering Opposition

One misconception is that teaching about oppression and shameful moments in U.S. history fosters reverse racism, guilt, and discomfort. PEN America (2022), an organization that has defended the free expression of ideas for over a century, reports that as of 2021, 24 states have passed laws forcing educators to omit discussions about "divisive concepts" and racism and to censor lessons about slavery and the genocide of Native peoples. For example, a school district in Texas instructed its teachers to balance having books on the Holocaust with those that hold "opposing views" (PEN America, 2022, p. 1).

The Learn from History Coalition (https://Learnfromhistory.org), a wide-ranging group that includes the National School Boards Association, the School Superintendents Association, the American Federation of Teachers, the National Council for Social Studies, and many educators recommends:

- educating parents/guardians and the public about what is taught in schools;
- explaining the importance of teaching accurate and fact-based history and that racism is wrong; and
- dramatizing in authentic, nonpolitical, nonconfrontational ways the harm of restricting what is taught in American schools.

 Reflection Task

1. Discuss 2–3 steps that you might take to follow the guidance from the Learn from History Coalition in partnering with families.
2. How can you explain to parents/guardians why students need to learn accurate portrayals of history?

LOOKING AHEAD

This chapter discussed the importance of supporting children's positive identity development, countering negative influences, and building and strengthening home-school partnerships. In the next chapter, we will explore ways to harness the power of connectedness, cooperation, and compassion to manifest their identities in the world and help them engage in identity safe relationships.

ADDITIONAL RESOURCES

- **Understanding Gender**
  Gender Spectrum. (n.d.). Introduction: Creating gender inclusive schools. https://www.genderspectrum.org/articles/cgis-introduction
- **Racial Trauma**
  Hardy, K. V. (2013). Healing the hidden wounds of racial trauma. *Reclaiming Children and Youth, 22*(1), 24–28. https://sfgov.org/juvprobation/sites/default/files/Documents/juvprobation/JPC_2014/Healing_the_Hidden_Wounds_of_Racial_Trauma.pdf
- **Developmentally Appropriate Conversations About Race and Gender**
  Cohn-Vargas, B., Kahn, A. C., Epstein, A., & Gogolewski, K. (2022). *Belonging and Inclusion in Identity Safe Schools: A Guide for Educational Leaders.* Appendix H (pp. 248–251). Corwin.
- **Supporting Student Empowerment**
  Zacarian, D., & Silverstone, M. A. (2020). What does an empowered student look like? In *Teaching to Empower: Taking Action to Foster Student Agency, Self-Confidence, and Collaboration* (pp. 7–22). ASCD.

CHAPTER 5

Harnessing the Power of Connectedness, Cooperation, and Compassion

One of my mom's favorite stories is about me in preschool. She begins the story by saying that as soon as she dropped me off, if I saw one kid crying, I would naturally go up to the kid and say, "It's okay. Your parents will be back soon."

One of my favorite stories about my mom is about when I had a conflict with my brothers and what she would say to me. It always went something like, "Why did you break his Lego?" And I would answer with something like, "Because I was mad at him." She responded, "How would you feel if your Lego was broken? Mad? Sad? Why do you think he feels mad? Sad?" She wouldn't reprimand us or say that we were bad. Instead, she'd tell us to try to understand the other person, what they were going through, and where they were coming from. And I realized, oh, man, if I was in their position, how would I feel? Promoting empathy was always her first instinct. She taught me that when you try to understand another person's feelings, more often than not, you'll find a mirror between you and this other person.

Daniel, the college student we met in Chapter 2

When children learn to cooperate with empathy and compassion, a classroom becomes more identity safe. In Chapter 2, we discussed the importance of creating a caring culture at school. In this chapter, we explore how to help children connect, cooperate, and become compassionate. We present the following:

- Foundations of cooperation, empathy, and compassion, and why they matter
- Research-based methods to reduce and eliminate prejudice and bias

- Strategies to help children develop understanding and stand up for themselves and others
- Home-school partnerships to promote social and emotional learning (SEL) and counter opposition to it

WHAT ARE CONNECTION, COOPERATION, AND COMPASSION, AND WHY DO THEY MATTER?

Children's social and emotional development and the capacity to relate to others emerge through home, school, and community interactions. The definition of social and emotional learning is:

> The processes through which all young people and adults acquire and apply the knowledge, skills, and attitudes to develop healthy identities, manage emotions and achieve personal and collective goals, feel and show empathy for others, establish and maintain supportive relationships, and make responsible and caring decisions. (CASEL, n.d.)

Identity safe relationships are cultivated through learning to be respectful, cooperative, and compassionate with the freedom for each person to express their authentic self.

Connections Through Positive and Collaborative Relationships

> Relationships based on mutual respect and dignity are foundational in identity safety. The need to belong and feel connected to others is a positive motivational force and a basic human need. Whether we are being nourished, motivated, and challenged or, conversely, angered, blamed, or hurt over and over again, our relationships are constantly shaping our perceptions, thoughts, and feelings (Steele, D. M. & Cohn-Vargas, 2013, p. 119).

Researchers have found that promoting cooperation results in "higher quality relationships, valuing heterogeneity" and "social competencies, shared identity, and the ability to cope with stress and adversity" (Johnson & Johnson, 2010, p. 203). In addition, cooperation is taught through formal cooperative structures, practiced throughout the school day, and integrated into all interactions (Steele, D. M. & Cohn-Vargas, 2013). The SISP study highlighted the components of cooperation and positive relationships as significant contributors to a child's sense of identity safety (Steele, D. M., 2012).

Fostering Empathy and Compassion

The Greater Good Science Center (n.d.) describes two types of empathy, affective and cognitive, as follows:

1. *Affective empathy* refers to the sensations and feelings we get in response to others' emotions; this can include mirroring what that person is feeling or feeling stressed when we detect another's fear or anxiety.
2. *Cognitive empathy*, sometimes called "perspective taking," refers to our ability to identify and understand other people's emotions. (para. 2)

Using functional magnetic resonance imaging (fMRI), researchers discovered mirror neurons. These brain cells trigger when we observe someone being pinched, as if the pain of being pinched is happening to us. In addition to sensing another person's physical pain, we have empathetic reactions to another person's feelings of joy, excitement, fear, anger, sadness, embarrassment, and disgust (Bernhardt & Singer, 2012). For example, mirror neurons explain why babies can be observed laughing, crying, and mimicking others (Winerman, 2005). However, the feeling of empathy does not guarantee that we want to help another person in a time of need. This is where compassion comes into focus.

Compassion is a sensitivity to the suffering of oneself and others and a commitment to alleviate it. Paul Gilbert (2015), compassion scholar, explains, "Compassion is not just about kindness or 'softness,' and it is certainly not a weakness—it is one of the most important declarations of strength and courage known to humanity" (para. 11). Compassion offers a way to interact in meaningful and fulfilling ways. It also draws on our innate tendencies toward caring for ourselves and others and our motivation to be free from the fear of threat. Very importantly, compassion is a force for healing the trauma and deep hurt that all people experience. Beyond seeking to alleviate personal suffering, compassionate action can extend to remediating inequitable systemic conditions that cause suffering.

Identity safe practices foster individual and interpersonal compassion and extend to working for systemic change grounded in equity. To achieve equity, all voices are heard, and multidiverse identities and multiple perspectives are honored. However, it also requires understanding prejudice and how to reduce it. It includes examining our implicit biases and intentionally working to address and eliminate them.

Reducing Prejudice and Implicit and Explicit Bias

Social psychologist Gordon Allport, author of the groundbreaking book *The Nature of Prejudice* (1954, 1958, 1979), identified four research-based ways to reduce prejudice.

1. Acquaintance potential: personal contact as people from different backgrounds connect in meaningful ways.
2. Equal status: efforts to level the playing field among different social groups.
3. Cooperative interdependence: people with different identities cooperating on a superordinate project while expressing their unique identities (e.g., cheering for a sports team).
4. Social and institutional support: Legitimization by authorities and leaders promoting equality through norms and laws that exist across an institution.

As explained in Chapter 1, identity safe environments honor authentic expression and do not aim to erase differences.

TAKING ACTION

A prerequisite for children and adults to engage in positive relationships is the capacity to be aware of and manage emotions. When we cooperate with others, we learn to work toward mutually beneficial goals. When we feel empathy and exercise compassion, we participate in the world in fulfilling and meaningful ways.

What we propose is a path to help children cultivate connection, cooperation, and compassion by:

- learning self-awareness by reading their body sensations and managing their emotions through self-regulation;
- strengthening interpersonal skills for communicating and collaborating; and
- helping children learn to speak up and stand up for themselves and others.

When we cultivate these prosocial capacities, we strengthen a child's emerging sense of belonging.

Cultivating Self-Awareness

Children develop an awareness of their feelings by learning to trust in their bodies, regulate emotions, control impulses, and manage moments of happiness and distress. Additionally, they can learn to describe what it feels like when they are appreciated and respected.

Psychologists and trauma specialists Peter Levine and Maggie Kline (2008) explain,

> The language of sensation is communicated from the deep recesses of the brain in what we shall call the "body-brain." Young children's prefrontal cortexes are not yet fully developed. As a result, they feel a sensation before their brains register what they are feeling and do not have the words to describe when something triggers an emotional reaction. Adults can help them learn to understand the language of their bodies. We can teach them simple ways to talk about their emotions. (p. 15)

Self-awareness related to safety and belonging grows when children learn to recognize bodily sensations. Self-awareness enables children to interact in positive ways. Carlee, the trauma-responsive practices facilitator we met in Chapter 4, describes how self-awareness occurs first on a somatic level. She also shares what she does to teach her own children how to recognize these feelings so that they can become more aware of the meaning behind the sensations they experience.

> Our bodies sense whether something feels good or not long before we have words to describe it. Even before we react, the first thing that happens is a felt sense. So, we can help children trust in the signals from their bodies, alerting them that something doesn't feel good. We can give them the language of sensation rather than emotion to describe the feeling, "I feel shaky, I feel cold, I feel hot, I feel off—rather than trying to say I don't feel safe."

> I teach my children to identify sensations in their bodies to help them discern what their bodies are telling them. At first, they don't have words for mad or sad, much less uncertain, or worried. However, they can tell when their stomach tightens, their face gets hot, or their heartbeat starts to go faster. They can describe sensations of tingly or hotness. In that instant, those sensations are more accessible. That can also be true for adults.

We can teach children to describe more abstract feelings like safety, belonging, and respect. Carlee, for example, teaches children to read the somatic signals from their bodies.

Children can sense that "my body knows I feel good when I feel respected when I feel safe."

We can ask, "What are the times when you felt most that way?"

A child might say, "When I am with my grandma, my puppy, or climbing a tree."

We can teach them that they can draw on those resources when they're upset or in an activated state. We tell them, "You can think about being with your grandma, your puppy, or when you climb that tree," . . . . We do this not to help distract them from feelings but to help resource emotions enough to get back—integrated into their bodies. As adults, we too can learn each other's signals for when we're not feeling a sense of safety, dignity, or belonging. This helps us get through tough moments. It can also help us develop empathy for others and recognize another person's ways of telling us they need support.

Adults can validate children's feelings and use activities to help them trust the language of their bodies. Levine and Kline (2008) recommend activities to build awareness of bodily sensations and help children describe feelings. Here are several examples.

Tree Exercise

- Children can act out being a tree, lifting their arms like branches extending into the air and roots deep into the ground. Then we ask them to describe how it felt, helping them get in touch with different bodily sensations.

Sensation Body Maps

- Introduce colors of the rainbow and match them to emotions (e.g., pink = happy, blue = sad, purple = energetic, red = mad). Practice talking about colors to indicate their feelings.
- Have children lie on butcher paper, draw the outline of their bodies, and use the colors to show where they feel different emotions in their bodies.

Draw a Safe Place

- Ask children to draw a picture of a safe place. Drawing helps children to express feelings that they may not be able to articulate. Then ask them to describe their pictures, putting their thoughts into words.

We can help children trust their bodies' signals, especially those related to safety and belonging. Then they can learn when to reach out and ask for help. Finally, we can help them build a bank of internal resources drawing from people who care about them, their community, and their culture.

Cultivating Self-Regulation

Self-regulation is our internal process of regulating emotions, which is essential for children's pro-social interactions with others. By regulating their emotions, they can soothe and calm themselves when triggered. This helps them to stop reacting impulsively or harm themselves or their peers.

Stuart Shanker (2016), a renowned research professor emeritus of philosophy and psychology at York University and expert in self-regulation, explains the connection between being able to calm oneself down and empathy,

> The absolute core of empathy is pure right brain-to-right brain communication in which we let our child feel we aren't abandoning her in her time of need. When we do this, we're activating positive memories lodged deep in her limbic systems from times when she was a baby, and Mommy's or Daddy's reassuring touch or voice took away the fear. A child not only is calmed in this way but, once calmed, will seek to reengage, and eventually extend empathy and receive it. (p. 198)

Trauma-responsive coach Carlee shares how she draws from Shanker's ideas with her own children. She teaches them to be present in the moment and prepares them to access and utilize their inner strengths.

> At dinner, we talk about the best part of our day and how it made us feel. We also share the most challenging part of our day and what we did to get through it. That helps them learn to reflect on how they can find resources in themselves and notice how they worked through something hard. My little toddler, Aleya, can talk about what she does to help herself, even without using the word help. It's cool. She'll say, "I asked for a hug from Frankie [her brother]."

Carlee also shares an important point about supporting children to feel their own emotions rather than ascribing what we perceive those emotions to be for them. She highlights one of the key components of identity safety, "listening to student voices," using behavioral supports when working with children.

> Often people try to tell children how they feel. They'll say, "It's okay. It wasn't so bad," to try to help them get over whatever happened. I don't

do that. I try not to tell them how they feel. First, I ask, "Are you okay? Do you want me to be with you, or do you want some space?" Often, they push away first, then reach out, so I wait for a clear signal that they want me close.

Many of Carlee's high school students have experienced multiple adversities (such as living in extreme poverty, having parents addicted to drugs, and witnessing gang violence in their neighborhoods).

> In my classroom, I used a weather or nature metaphor to ask, "What kind of weather do you feel on the inside today, or what animal do you feel like today?" That helped them give me a picture rather than a judgment. For example, a student who was feeling bad might have described it as cloudy. I'd be sure to check in with that student during class or at the end to see if it had changed. This allowed them to start referencing their inner experience as something that was not static.

The unpredictable phenomena of abuse, neglect, and household challenges may lead to a prolonged sense of uncertainty and, in turn, chronic stress and anxiety. A way to mitigate such outcomes is by helping students to draw from their inner strengths to engage and recognize their capacity to cope (Zacarian et al., 2017).

Cultivating Our Own Self-Compassion and Regulation

The process of helping children to self-regulate cannot be separated from efforts to manage our own emotions as parents/guardians and educators, nor should it! Levine and Kline (2008) explain "the experiential knowledge of sensations will not only give you the tools to assist your overwhelmed child; it has the side benefit of helping you, the parents, avoid becoming distraught as well" (p. 15). We can do this by practicing kindness and compassion toward ourselves daily, reflecting on our reactions to others and ourselves.

Self-compassion is not weakness or selfishness. Kristin Neff is an associate professor of educational psychology at the University of Texas–Austin and the author of books and articles on self-compassion. Neff (2012) explains that self-compassion requires

> self-kindness, as opposed to self-judgment. . . . So self-compassion involves being warm and supportive—actively soothing ourselves. The second part is remembering that imperfection is part of the shared human experience—that you're not alone in your suffering. . . . The third component is mindfulness. If you aren't mindfully aware that you're suffering, if you're just

repressing your pain or ignoring it or getting lost in problem-solving, you can't give yourself compassion. (para. 9)

We can strengthen our capacity for self-compassion and draw upon our resources for empathy when children frustrate us with oppositional behavior, fighting, or temper tantrums. That allows us to focus on our love for them. That way, we can address their behavior rather than make them feel shame or bad for disappointing us. Often their defiance means they are seeking safety. Indeed, some repeated behaviors are a cry for help. Carlee offers strategies for modeling self-compassion for children:

> Inevitably there will be times when we act in ways that we are not proud of, but we can let children know our behavior is not because of them *and* that we are seeking a better strategy. We can intentionally practice compassion, forgiveness, and gratitude daily. By modeling humility to our children, they learn to forgive themselves for mistakes as we continually manifest values of care and love.

Along with internal capacities, we foster interpersonal skills to help children attune themselves to the people around them and learn to communicate, collaborate, and solve problems.

Cooperating and Honoring Interdependence

When children feel valued as part of a group, they feel connected to one another and have a sense of belonging. Educators can build a culture of interdependence where everyone cares for each other with classroom norms based on children helping each other to ensure everybody learns. The type of mistake-safe culture we discussed in Chapter 2 fosters trust. It serves to promote a child's growth mindset, where they grow smarter by exerting effort and learn from making mistakes (Dweck, 2006).

In Chapter 2, we also highlighted Hofstede's (2011) and Hofestede et al.'s (2005) research on collectivist cultures where cooperation is fundamental to family and community life. Many of our students come from cultures with a tradition of communal values (e.g., African American, Native American, Latinx, Asian, and Middle Eastern). Mary Murphy, Indiana University professor of psychological and brain sciences, researches stereotype threat and the growth mindset in the context of schools and organizations. Mary Murphy describes the importance of interdependence in a community of learners.

> [Educators can make] more space for students from interdependent backgrounds that are more focused on community, roles, relationships, and

responsibilities. [We can foster] a culturally inclusive growth mindset culture, [which involves using] a growth mindset through an inclusive, inter-dependent lens. . . . [where] teachers use "we" rather than "you" and "I" language. That actually has the benefit of creating a non-competitive learning culture in the classroom and motivating students from interdependent backgrounds. They feel their background fits the classroom more than an independent space where it is just about me showing my smarts as an individual. . . . It is the idea that, as a classroom community, we are working together as a team to grow our brains and increase our capabilities. (M. Murphy, personal communication, 2018)

By fostering a *culturally inclusive growth mindset culture*, interdependence is infused into the dynamics of a school, and educators communicate to children (1) that we are all in this together and (2) that we will not leave anyone behind. We can encourage students to turn to peers when they are stuck or need help understanding a concept. An emphasis on cooperation at the personal and systemic levels helps children feel more identity safe and connected to one another.

Reflection Task

Reflect on Creating a Culturally Inclusive Growth Mindset:

1. Describe 1–2 examples of ways you engage children in cooperation and interdependence.
2. How do the examples you shared relate to the points that Murphy makes?

Reducing Bias and Prejudice: A Tool for Embracing Diversity

As we foster identity safety, we seek to reduce prejudices and biases at home and school. Children can engage in activities to learn about themselves and one another at all grade levels. Younger children can share family stories and traditions. As students mature, they can learn about their many social identities, interview family members, and share about their identities. These activities enhance empathy as children build relationships with their multidiverse peers.

When engaging in personal sharing, an important caveat is that we can inadvertently undermine efforts by asking students to self-disclose too much and take risks with others they hardly know. For example, in

Chapter 1, Vinnie shared the experiences he had being bullied for not fitting in with gender norms. In another incident in 2nd grade, his peers teased him, calling him a girl. Intending to promote empathy, the teacher brought him together with those doing the name-calling. Then she asked Vinnie to describe how he felt. Vinnie complied. Immediately after, the children made fun of what he said and continued bullying him. This pain lingered for Vinnie for years. The teacher never knew the harm she caused.

In another example, a middle school principal, in an effort to increase awareness and support for LGBTQ+ identities, organized an awareness day where students were instructed to self-identify in groups as cisgender, gender nonconforming, or unsure. However, students reported feeling unsafe when forced to expose themselves during the activity.

For group activities, carefully consider how students might feel as they engage in the activities we prepare.

- *Might the activity cause embarrassment in any way?* For example, when holding a birthday party with students from different economic backgrounds, avoid opening presents, making those with humbler gifts or no gifts feel awkward.
- *Might the activities require students to have prior personal, cultural, linguistic, or academic knowledge to participate?* For example, children may be encouraged to play "four square" and there may be a child in the group unfamiliar with the game. Take steps to ensure that every student can participate with the depth of knowledge needed to play at the various levels (e.g., beginning, advanced beginning, and so forth).
- *If an activity includes a form of personal sharing, consider giving options for them to choose whether they want to share and what they feel comfortable saying.* For example, when asking students to describe bullying, how might they share something they witnessed or experienced personally without naming any names?
- *Will the activities require a child to listen, speak, read, or write in a target language?* Take steps to support children who are not yet able to communicate with peers who are fluent in that language. For example, if the expectation is that an activity will occur in English, a student who speaks a language other than English might be supported by a translator, parent, or multilingual peer.

Taking Compassionate Action as Allies and Upstanders

Children can exercise compassion and solidarity by learning to be allies and upstanders. An ally supports another person whether or not they share that person's or group's identity. Allies consider the needs of the person they are supporting, being careful not to dominate or overshadow them. Chen, whom we met in Chapter 4, recalls how her teacher noticed when Chen acted as an ally supporting a new student and rewarded her for doing so.

> My PE teacher would select a student for recognition at the end of the year. When she selected me, I was surprised because I wasn't the fastest athlete, but I think she'd been watching me. It was nice that she acknowledged my efforts to be inclusive. I thought that's what every kid was supposed to do. My teacher's influence shaped me to be intentional in my work as an educator. I try to notice who is at the table and create space and opportunity for contributions from those who are not traditionally part of the conversation.

What Is an Upstander?

The Oxford English Dictionary defines an upstander as "a person who speaks or acts in support of an individual or cause, particularly someone who intervenes on behalf of a person being attacked or bullied" (Stevenson, 2015). In identity safety, we seek to empower students as upstanders when they speak up for others and *themselves*.

In 2014, I (Becki) worked with Monica Mahal and Sarah Decker, two high school students leading a districtwide bullying prevention campaign in New Jersey. The following year, as college students, they mounted a campaign to get the word upstander into the dictionary. In their words (Decker & Mahal, 2014),

> An upstander is an individual who sees wrong and acts, and the most important part is that anyone can become one. . . . The word itself [can] empower students to make an active change in their schools in an effort to build communities that support difference and unify against intolerance. (para. 2)

We can teach students to be upstanders through discussions and pointing out examples, inviting children to share their own experiences. We can present age-appropriate scenarios. For example, younger students can role-play bullying, teasing, and name-calling and propose solutions. Middle and high school students can practice speaking up when they hear a racial or homophobic slur. We can explain how to intervene safely and get help from a trusted adult when necessary. When a bullying incident occurs, children can reflect on their actions. Especially those who were bystanders can consider how to be upstanders.

Children can be upstanders at school and home. For example, Vinnie relates that during his childhood, his mother worked, and often, he and his siblings were home without adult supervision. At those times, Vinnie's brother repeatedly taunted, teased, and bullied him.

> My brother was four years older than me and my biggest bully. I would experience awful violence at home. Thank goodness for my older sister, who was one year younger than my brother. She would come to my defense. She would get in his face and tell him to stop. I honestly do not know what I would have done without my sister. She was my savior.

Shining a Light on Standing Up for Oneself

We met Lenore in Chapter 4. Here, she describes how her son Emmanuel came to learn how to stand up for himself in 4th grade.

There were only two Black boys in Emmanuel's class, and he had a support teacher, not his primary teacher, who kept calling him by the other young man's name for the entire year. He complained to me, and I suggested we talk to the teacher about it. He said, "Nope. I don't want you to do anything."

So, I replied, "Then why are you complaining? Either we do something about it, or you will have to suck it up." However, he was adamant that he didn't want to. So, finally, two weeks before the school year was over, he said to me, "I'm done. If she calls me by his name again, I'm gonna let her know."

I said, "Wait, let me talk to the head of school before you go there." I didn't want him to lose his temper. So, I tried to call the head of school, but she didn't get back to me in time. Later, when I picked him up from school, he got in the car and said, "I told her. I didn't even lose my temper or raise my voice. I stayed calm and said, 'You keep calling me by so and so's name, and I don't like it. My name is Emmanuel.' And she said, 'I'm so sorry. I didn't mean to do that.' So, I told her, 'I know, you didn't mean to do it. But you keep doing it. And I think it's racist because we are the only two Black kids in the class. You call everyone else by their names, but not me and him.'"

He was articulate, calm, and thorough in explaining to her why this was bothering him and why he felt that it was racist. It did my heart good and made me feel he is going to be okay. He was able to be an advocate for himself in such an impressive manner, making me very proud of him.

Reflection Task

Reflect on Upstanders and Allies:

> Consider the earlier examples from Chen, Vinnie, and Lenore that show how educators, students, and families can stand up for themselves and one another as you answer the following questions.

1. Has anyone ever stood up for you?
   - If yes, describe was happened and how you felt before, during, and after the incident.
   - If not, was there ever a time you wished someone had stood up for you?
2. Have you ever had to stand up for yourself either as a child or an adult? Describe what happened and how it made you feel.
3. Think of a time when you were an ally or upstander. Describe the experience, how it felt, and the result. What did you learn?
4. How might you teach and support children and youth to become allies and upstanders?

PARTNERSHIPS WITH HOME AND SCHOOL

In this section, we examine partnerships to support cooperation and compassion, including

- home and schools working together to address implicit biases;
- schools helping parents/guardians support LGBTQ+ youth; and
- positively countering opposition to SEL by informing parents/guardians about why SEL is important for their children.

Addressing Implicit Bias

In Chapter 3, we discussed how in a society rife with stereotypes about different racial and gender identities, we are all subject to biases, leading to unconscious attitudes. We asked you to consider your unconscious biases. Here we examine how parents/guardians and educators can partner to respond to and address bias.

Shining a Light on Our Beliefs About Implicit Bias

We met Susan in Chapter 1, where she explained that she and her husband, Jeff, were careful to protect their four daughters from bias after moving to the United States from Dominica.

> My husband, Jeff, and I attended a parent conference with Vignetta's 3rd-grade teacher. She was a wonderful lady praising how smart Vignetta was, pointing to Vignetta's writing, posted along with the work of another student under a sign saying, "Our Best Work." Jeff scrutinized the bulletin board and noticed that the one next to Vignetta's had the word "excellent" written on it while Vignetta's did not. So, Jeff asked, "What's wrong with her work? Why doesn't Vignetta's paper say excellent too?" Then Jeff added, "I bet that one belongs to a little White boy."
>
> "Yes," the teacher replied, growing embarrassed. So, Jeff told her, "Please either take Vignetta's down or write 'excellent' on hers too. Because right now, you're sending her a message that her work is very good, but it's not excellent compared to the boy's work." So, the teacher stood up and wrote "excellent" on it.

This was not an isolated incident for Susan and Jeff. They reported frequent incidents that signaled lowered expectations about their daughters' intelligence and academic skills.

> When one of our daughters walked into her honors math class on the first day of school, she was the only Black student. The teacher mistakenly told her she was in the wrong room, even though it was her correct classroom and she had been a top math student.
>
> Our other daughter's counselor suggested she attend a dental hygiene program at the community college, ignoring her high grades and desire to become a dentist or a doctor.
>
> Jeff and I would march right over each time to confront and resolve the issues. These teachers loved our daughters and were mortified that they had not even realized they were doing these things. That is the sadness of it.
>
> I always tell other parents, "You cannot just leave your children and hope for the best because stereotyping and bias are real."

Reflection Task

Reflect on what can be done to stop implicit biases from harming students.

1. Why did Jeff feel it necessary for the teacher to add the word "excellent" to his daughter's paper?

2. What would you have said to the teachers if you were in any situations Susan and Jeff's daughters experienced?

3. How might you have responded if you were one of Susan and Jeff's daughters' teachers?

In addition to implicit bias resulting in lowered academic expectations for students of color, biases lead to unfair discipline practices. For example, studies have shown that Black boys are more severely disciplined than White boys for similar behavior (Eberhardt et al., 2004). Further, the juvenile justice system continuously shows substantial disparities between White youth and youth of color. Recent data indicates that the latter group face higher odds of juvenile court involvement, detention, formal prosecution, and adult charges compared to the former group (National Academies of Science, Engineering, and Medicine, 2022).

Shining Another Light on Implicit Bias

Our second example explores what happens when a child is subjected to implicit bias in kindergarten. Laura is White and married to an African American man, and they have two sons. Her younger son experienced an incident with extremely negative ramifications during the first weeks of school.

This happened in the school cafeteria during Max's second week of kindergarten. On Friday, my son was sitting with some boys and girls at the lunch table, and children of all genders were looking up each other's pants. They were clowning around and saying inappropriate things. One little girl went home and told her parents what happened, only singling out Max, although all the kids at that table were participating. The following Monday, the girl's parents complained to the principal. Then the principal and my son's teacher spoke with Max using adult terminology for a person who sexually assaulted someone, requiring him to keep his hands to himself and giving him consequences.

My son, who had just turned 5, was basically treated like a criminal, as if he'd sexually assaulted the girl. Later, I learned that the incident had already been handled immediately in the lunchroom. There, one of the teachers used age-appropriate language to tell the children why they should not engage in this behavior. However, neither the classroom teacher nor the principal investigated what happened that day in the lunchroom.

> My son had participated in something inappropriate, but as an innocent child who didn't know better, and he wasn't the only one. After that, his teacher started treating him differently. This experience quite honestly ruined his relationship with school, and he began having trouble in the classroom.

Laura believes that implicit bias influenced the overreaction of the principal and classroom teacher. Most likely, they were unaware that they unfairly targeted a Black child playing into age-old pernicious stereotypes about Black men as sexual predators.

 Reflection Task

1. How might Laura approach the principal and teacher to help them become aware of and address the implicit bias her son experienced?
2. What are some additional examples of implicit bias that you have observed or experienced? How were these handled successfully, or how might these be handled more successfully?
3. How would you respond if someone told you that an action you took was biased?

Being vigilant requires that we notice and remedy situations of bias. It necessitates that parents/guardians and school personnel work closely together.

For parents/guardians,

- listen to your child's version of what happened and observe their demeanor and reactions, then, consider the longer-range implications of each situation;
- address concerns with school personnel with a translator or parent advocate if needed; and
- request long-range solutions.

For educators,

- notice when biases occur;
- listen without being defensive, be willing to investigate fairly, and acknowledge when errors have been made and rectify them;
- monitor that the situation does not continue and work to rebuild trust;

- examine behavioral and academic data to look for patterns at your school site and work to rectify systemic policies and practices;
- educate the staff on ways to reduce implicit and explicit biases; and
- continue to self-reflect on your own biases and work to eliminate them.

Shining a Light on a Parent's Journey to Support Her Daughter

We met Sonia in Chapter 3, where we learned how her child, assigned male at birth, announced she was a girl at the age of 6. We described how Sonia and her husband supported their child, including changing her name to the now pre-ferred feminine name of Sheila. However, after helping family members accept her daughter Sheila's gender transition, Sonia faced even greater roadblocks at school.

> Although our family lived in a conservative area, I was under the impression that if I just explained things and provided resources, wouldn't the school want to help?

At the start of 2nd grade, shortly after Sheila announced that she was a girl, Sonia approached the private school principal to share the steps that she was taking at home and the actions needed at school to support her child. She also provided the principal with information about state and federal laws to ensure equitable treatment of transgender children like Sheila.

> Several months after our initial conversation, the principal of that private school contacted me to say, "Your child can't come here to this school next year, identify-ing as a girl." Also, students began bullying Sheila. That February, Sheila asked her grandma what suicide was and what would happen if she suicided herself. When I heard this, I pulled her out of school that day.

Sonia stopped working and homeschooled Sheila for the remainder of the school year. She focused on ensuring that Sheila felt safe. Then she found a public school where she felt Sheila would be supported.

> At the start of the year, at a PTA meeting on back-to-school night, a man stood up and said, "I want to talk about the fact that there is going to be a boy in the girl's bathroom this year, the state of California is saying that boys can use the girl's bath-rooms, and that is happening right now at our school."

The principal was not present when this happened. The man and his wife had a small group of supporters who continued protesting Sheila's legal right to use the girl's bathroom. However, most of the parents supported Sheila and Sonia's family.

> After that night, many women came up to me and said, "We have your back. Hell no, we are not okay with people treating kids that way." So, I joined the PTA; I became a super volunteer so that people would love us, so they wouldn't turn on us. It's so sad, but it worked. My daughters and I ended up having a huge support system, including lunch and playground ladies who just adopted us.

                Reflection Task

1. As the school principal at a parent meeting, how might you respond to a parent/guardian who makes a deficit-based statement about a group of students or families?
2. What do you believe Sonia meant by the phrase, "super volunteer"? How might you support others (including those who might be reluctant or unable to volunteer) to engage in the same behaviors as Sonia?
3. What would you do to reach out to families of marginalized students and involve them in the school?

Sonia continues to fight for Sheila's safety and inclusion. However, she is happy to have found a middle school committed to collaborating with her to support Sheila's education. Six years later, Sonia joyously describes her daughter, who is now 13.

> Sheila's amazing. So resilient and so smart. Sheila has a ton of friends and got straight A-pluses this quarter. Sheila's independent and strong and smart and just gorgeous.

Educating Parents/Guardians to Support LGBTQ+ Youth

Schools can play an essential role in supporting LGBTQ+ students when a child's parents/guardians are not supporting them. As described in Chapter 1, LGBTQ+ youth whom family members and caregivers reject are more likely to attempt suicide (Ryan et al., 2010). Vinnie explains how schools can help change parent/guardian attitudes.

> A child who feels unsafe at home cannot learn. If they are not well, students cannot learn, especially if they contemplate self-harm or suicide. We can

help families get on that journey to support their children and help parents/guardians move from rejecting to less rejecting, to neutral to accepting. This will significantly decrease suicide ideation. Many families have been exposed to misinformation about what LGBTQ+ means because opponents often falsely sexualize it. Parents/guardians worry that their kids will be sexualized or recruited to be LGBTQ at a young age. For clarity, people don't choose to be LGBTQ just as they don't choose to be straight or cisgender.

Vinnie has worked as a teacher, school counselor, and national leader at the Human Rights Campaign, supporting LGBTQ+ youth and families.

While school counselors are there to support students, I believe that part of their job is to help families support their children. When a young person tells their school counselor that their family has rejected them, they can work with the student to find an effective way to help. By scheduling a meeting with a child's family, school counselors can help parents/guardians understand their child and begin a slow process toward family acceptance. When parents/guardians understand the dangers and suicide risks for a child whose family rejects them, they often pause because they certainly do not want their child to have suicidal thoughts. As a school counselor, I've had many of those conversations. These meetings have been very helpful in getting that family to begin the journey of supporting their child. It's certainly not an overnight thing. It's a journey. I keep saying journey on purpose. However, getting on that journey is essential. Moreover, I believe educators play a critical role in helping make that happen.

Here are Vinnie's suggestions for things schools can do:

- Create an LGBTQ+ resource page on their website with culturally varied links to LGBTQ+ tools for families to learn about LGBTQ+ inclusion.
- Provide educational sessions for parents/guardians to educate about LGBTQ+ inclusion with data and research-based identity safety practices for LGBTQ+ students.
- Inform parents/guardians how to proactively let children know they support LGBTQ+ relatives or friends when they see an LGBTQ+ character in a television show. This sends a subliminal message of support to children rather than leaving their children guessing or imagining whether their caregivers are supportive.
- Connect families to resources and organizations like PFLAG (https://pflag.org), a national nonprofit organization offering

> monthly support groups for parents/guardians with LGBTQ+ children. PFLAG has chapters all across the United States.

In his article "Responding to Pushback" for the American School Counselor Association, Vinnie writes,

> School counselors understand that societal views of LGBTQ+ people continue to be fueled by an abundance of misinformation, stigma, and negative biases. It is incumbent on all educators to proactively address negative biases about differences; they hinder the learning process and affect students' mental wellness. . . . The ASCA Ethical Standards for School Counselors call on us to "support all students and their development by actively working to eliminate systemic barriers or bias impeding student development." (Pompei, 2022)

Vinnie's points are especially true about such critical topics as collaboration and communication, included among a robust set of 21st-century skills (Bellanca & Brandt, 2010).

Protection of Student Privacy

Family rejection, as we cited earlier (Ryan et al., 2010), has been found to be the most significant factor influencing suicide ideation and completed suicides for LBGTQ+ youth. As such, it is critical to be well-informed about the protection of student privacy. Guidance from the American Civil Liberties Union (Esseks, 2020) offers important insights.

> Students have the constitutional right to share or withhold information about their sexual orientation or gender identity from their parents, teachers, and other parties, and it is against the law for school officials to disclose or compel students to disclose that information. Even when students appear to be open about their sexual orientation or gender identity at school, it remains the student's right to limit the extent to which and with whom the information is shared. C.N. v. Wolf, 410 F. Supp. 2d 894, 903 (C.D. Cal. 2005) ("[T]the fact that an event is not wholly private does not mean that an individual has no interest in limiting disclosure or dissemination of that information to others."). The Family Educational Rights and Privacy Act ("FERPA") also protects students against the disclosure of personally identifiable information. (para. 3)

It is also critical to be well-informed of state laws and regulations regarding the protection of student privacy.

Positively Countering Opposition

Few people would oppose our providing instruction about listening to others, having empathy for others, mediating emotions, recognizing our own assets and strengths (and those of others), and resolving conflict in a productive matter (Zacarian et al., 2017). It is unlikely that any of us would argue against the value these skills play in one's development as a classroom, school, or family member, as well as a good citizen in a local community and beyond. The need for developing these skills is amplified every time there is a conflict in school, ranging from polite disagreement to a heated dispute or violent incident. Nevertheless, the Florida Department of Education has prohibited educators from providing instruction in social–emotional learning, social justice, and critical race theory (Anderson, 2022). Their core argument is that "these are unsolicited theories that may lead to student indoctrination and should, therefore, be prohibited" (Anderson, 2022).

SEL is the opposite of indoctrination! It should be included in all classroom settings—especially because its primary goal is to help young people think for themselves and make wise decisions. Further, a meta-analysis of 200 SEL programs in the United States demonstrated its value in improving behavior and academic achievement (Durlak et al., 2011). These findings were amplified in longitudinal studies conducted in rural and urban settings that found that students who received instruction in SEL had a greater chance of graduating from high school, completing college, and not having criminal records (Taylor et al., 2017). We all need to use the data described above to counteract misinformation about SEL and reinforce the social and citizenry benefits of social–emotional development and its relationship to ensuring the identity safety of an ever-growing populace of multidiverse learners.

LOOKING AHEAD

In this chapter, we explored ways to promote cooperation, compassion, and SEL while eliminating prejudice and bias to enhance a child's capacity to connect positively with others. In Chapter 6, we will show how fostering autonomy and resilience will empower students with agency on the path to identity safety.

ADDITIONAL RESOURCES

- **Self-Regulation**
  Shanker, S. (2016). *Self-reg: How to help your child (and you) break the stress cycle and successfully engage with life*. Penguin Press.

- **Modeling Empowerment**
  Zacarian, D., & Silverstone, M. A. (2020). Starting with ourselves. (Chapter 2). In *Teaching to empower: Taking action to foster student agency, self-confidence, and collaboration*. ASCD.
- **Supporting LGBTQ+ Students**
  Pompei, V. (2019). *LGBTQ youth: An educators guide* (2nd Edition). National Professional Resources, Inc.

CHAPTER 6

Building Empowerment, Agency, and Resilience

My son Matthew is a 7th-grade student in a public school system in a small New England community. He is on the autism spectrum and has a diagnosis of ADHD. Matthew struggles at school and performs significantly below grade level in several areas, including reading comprehension. In 3rd grade, his teacher recognized how challenging it was for Matthew to participate in class during story time. She knew that this was an especially difficult activity for him, but she also knew that Matthew was extremely motivated by rewards-based programs and loved Star Wars and puzzles. So, with our permission, she came up with a program to help motivate Matthew's participation, which also gave him a stronger sense of confidence and helped him feel more included in the class during story time. Every week, she printed out pictures of Matthew's favorite Star Wars characters and then cut these images into puzzle pieces. At story time, she would engage Matthew in the class discussion, and if he participated, she would later (privately) reward him with a single puzzle piece. At the end of each week, Matthew would work to collect all the pieces to complete the puzzle. Matthew would proudly bring home his personalized, completed puzzle each week. This program helped Matthew build the confidence to participate more in class (motivated by reward) and as such, feel an even greater sense of belonging by being part of class discussions during story time. Over the school year, the puzzles got larger, and Matthew would have to wait longer and answer more questions to complete his puzzles. One of the reasons this program was so successful was because it could evolve and keep Matthew motivated through the duration of the school year.

Rebecca, parent of a middle school student.

Educators and families may have different opinions about what works to support a child's learning. However, we all aspire to one unifying and overriding belief: we want children to succeed in school and in their lives. Foundational to our thinking about the possibilities of all young people realizing the gifts that identity safety brings is what we can do to address longstanding structural inequities and our own biases. We say this as our goal is for all families and educators to empower children to succeed in our ever-changing society. It requires that we support them to engage in environments where "cooperation, self-direction, self-reliance, communication, and interdependence is the norm" (Zacarian & Silverstone, 2020, p. 1). In Chapter 5, we discussed cooperation and the value of learning to work with others to foster a sense of belonging. This chapter explores empowerment as a way to draw on each child's unique assets.

In the example we introduced at the start of this chapter, notice how Rebecca, the mother of Matthew, and her son's teacher worked together to support his success in school. Looking at this through an empowerment lens helps us to rethink the positive possibilities of what we can do when we lay the groundwork for students to be autonomous learners, a key component of the SISP study (Steele, D. M. & Cohn-Vargas, 2013). In this chapter, we explore the following:

- What are empowerment, agency, and resilience, and why are they important?
- What can teachers and educators do to support a child's development to be empowered, have agency, and be resilient?
- Partnerships between home and school.

WHAT ARE EMPOWERMENT, AGENCY, AND RESILIENCE, AND WHY DO THEY MATTER?

A discussion about identity safety would not be complete without considering the actions that we take to empower children to have a voice and choice, which many refer to as agency. An example of such actions comes from one of our coauthors, Debbie, who served on the faculty at the University of Massachusetts, where she taught graduate and doctoral students to explore and research the concept of student empowerment in a course titled Managing Culturally Responsive Classrooms. During the first class of the semester, Debbie asked students to describe what an empowered learner looks like. Many invoked descriptions of people they knew, such as a sibling, someone they went to school with, and others who embodied, at least for them, the attributes of someone who has agency. We then unpacked some of the attributes that such people possess.

Empowerment and Agency

Historically, if we look back to the founding of American Public Schools, we learn that students were expected to learn by being quiet and strictly attending to their teachers as the sole source of the information needed to learn (Cohen, 1988). Back then, society reflected this type of ideology where children were expected to be obedient and follow the tenets espoused by their families and educators. We might call this a time when students were considered empty vessels, and it was their duty to pay unquestionable attention to their teacher. Almost a century later, John Dewey (1938) contributed significantly to what we now call *collaborative learning*. Students are expected to be much more contributory and participatory in their education.

Figure 6.1, adapted from Zacarian and Silverstone (2020), contains descriptors of an empowered student. While it is not a complete list, it provides the types of traits that we expect students to demonstrate when we reduce our authority as the sole purveyors of learning.

Reflection Task

Take a moment to think about the example we furnished at the beginning of this chapter of Rebecca, her son, Matthew, and Matthew's teacher.

1. Draw from Figure 6.1 and list 2–3 attributes you believe Matthew demonstrated.
2. Use the list you just created to write two to three sentences detailing what Matthew did to be an empowered learner.
3. Refer to Figure 6.1 and add four additional terms, words, idioms, or phrases (what Debbie calls TWIPs) to the list that you believe encompass the attributes of an empowered learner.

Figure 6.1. Descriptors of Empowered Student

action-oriented	flexible	observant	self-controlled
adaptable	generous	open-minded	validating
collaborative	independent	passionate	valued
contributory	insightful	reflective	wise
controls (mediates)	knowledgeable	resolves conflict	witty
emotions	mindful	productively	worthy
courageous	nonjudgmental	respectful	
creative		resilient	
determined			

When we (Debbie and Becki) did this task, we agreed that Matthew was determined to earn the puzzle pieces. We added the words *perseverant* and *motivated* to the list. However, we also noted something else. For Matthew to participate in class, he also had to be willing to (1) assert himself into the classroom conversation, (2) be respectful of others, all the while (3) engage in a level of self-control. You, our readers, may have noted the term self-control from Figure 6.1 and added the word *assertive* to the list of empowered attributes that Matthew exhibited. Empowerment, in today's classrooms at least, requires students to be autonomous and collaborative and actively contribute and even advocate on behalf of themselves and others (Zacarian & Silverstone, 2020). In the SISP study, the components "listening for student voices" and "classroom autonomy" emerged as important ways for educators to facilitate students in developing the skill of assertiveness (Steele, D. M. & Cohn-Vargas, 2013). Without question, families can and do play a significant role in helping their children become autonomous and empowered.

The specific skills that all students need to develop to be empowered and have agency vary from person to person and the context in which interactions occur. The length of time it takes to become empowered also varies. Consider, for example, that we are students in a middle school, and we go to our physical education class where our teacher is a prior college football player at a *top 10* university of the best football players in the country. He is planning to teach us how to play flag football. One classmate, the smartest mathematics student in our class, says, "I have never played the game. I hope he doesn't call on me!" In our hypothetical example, consider all the actions that this teacher takes.

Our class goes to the football field, and our teacher asks us to watch him throw the ball. After watching our teacher model this throw five times, he hands our classmate, the one who told us that she did not want to be singled out, the ball. We watch carefully. Our teacher respectfully makes some suggestions about where our classmate should hold her legs, arms, and hands, and after a few suggestions and much encouragement, our classmate prepares to launch the first throw. It drops from her hands. Observing her carefully, our teacher sees that our classmate is red-faced, and her eyes are now downcast. The teacher says:

> That is okay; we all have to learn. I was once a beginner and dropped the ball a hundred times. I still do! You are seeing me on a good day! Let's try again; this time, hold the ball like this, and let's see if it will go farther than your last throw. If it doesn't, I will adjust my suggestions.

We see our classmate make new adjustments and even smile! Next, our teacher models some additional suggestions with his arms and hands. Our

Figure 6.2. Skills of Receptiveness and Assertiveness

Receptiveness	Assertiveness
• Listens carefully to a speaker using context-specific communication and body language that indicates a high level of receptiveness to others. • Observes what the speaker says, models, or references. • Pays attention to the needs, ideas, and feelings of others in addition to oneself. • Finds the right time to speak. • Looks for common ground to make contributions that are positively additive rather than negatively subtractive.	• Counters ideas, needs, and desires respectfully. • Formulates ideas, desires, and feelings independently. • Articulates an idea, need, or desire. • Defends and modifies an idea. • Anticipates obstacles or barriers and addresses them with others in a respectful way.

Adapted from Zacarian and Silverstone (2020), pp. 127–129.

classmate carefully follows his instructions. Finally, we watch our classmate try again, and the ball miraculously (to us, at least) launches up in the air to the right and lands 10 feet away. In reaction, our teacher applauds her effort, affirms what she has done, and encourages her to throw the ball a third time. By the fifth trial and with positive feedback from our teacher and us, she launches the ball 10 yards. We congratulate her again!

In this context, our classmate's level of empowerment as a football player is far more at the beginning level of the spectrum than the proficient level of our teacher. While this example of our classmate's pre-emerging prowess as a football player might seem obvious, we are using it to show the spectrum of empowerment development.

Take a moment to look more closely at our hypothetical example of being taught to throw a football. The teacher observed our classmate carefully. He used language that expressed what he wanted his student to do while at the same time showing his respect for her. Being empowered involves the type of back-and-forth communication that requires us to modulate our level of assertiveness with and receptivity toward others. Figure 6.2 provides us with a list of some of the hallmarks of the two.

     Reflection Task

Reflect on Receptiveness and Assertiveness:

Consider the example furnished about our physical education teacher's receptiveness and assertiveness in being our teacher.

1. Drawing from Figure 6.2, list the receptive and assertive skills that our teacher demonstrated.
2. How might these guide you in planning empowerment instruction?

Considering Barriers to Empowerment and Agency

Before moving forward with a discussion about identity safety as it relates to empowerment, agency, and resilience, it is essential to acknowledge the longstanding and emerging barriers to empowerment that too many multidiverse students experience. These barriers undermine a child's confidence and hinder the process of becoming empowered and identity safe. An example might include students who have become proficient in English yet continue to be treated as if they are learning English. A second example might include a student with physical disabilities who rarely, if ever, is included in social play at recess with her peers. Inclusion and acceptance involves our looking closely and strategically at the steps we can take to support and embrace the empowerment efforts of all our students, their families, ourselves, and others.

Another example is college student Sameer, whom we met in Chapter 2. Like each of us, Sameer has multiple frames of reference for his identity. One is his frame of reference as a South Asian who was reared in a community composed almost entirely of people from the same ethnicity and culture as his. As you read the excerpt, think about the comfort that Sameer felt being reared in this environment.

> I grew up in Fremont, California, a large suburb in the Bay Area with a vast South Asian community. The city is around 50% Asian, and the neighborhood where I grew up was around 90% Asian. So, I never really felt different because of my cultural background, my skin color, the traditions that I celebrated, and the language that I spoke. Those all were very common amongst my peers growing up. Most of the people I went to school with growing up were also children of immigrants like me. So, in that sense, I was able to develop pride in my cultural background from a very young age. . . . And I got to learn a lot about my cultural background. It was a place where I felt very safe and very comfortable in that part of my identity.

As Sameer entered the 2nd grade, however, he noticed some differences between himself and his classmates. He also began being bullied for the succeeding 7 years.

As I started to get into, maybe, 2nd or 3rd grade, I felt like I had to have more boys as friends because there was more gender segregation going on where girls were friends with girls and boys were friends with boys. And when I had friends who were boys, they often didn't like any of the stuff or at least outwardly didn't like any of the stuff I liked. They enjoyed sports and rough play, and very violent video games. I didn't like any of those things and felt I had to hide what I did like because it was something that they would tease me for. Eventually, the bullying began.

I remember having to hide all my dolls under my bed anytime these friends would come over. Also, I remember my parents would ask, "Why do you feel like you have to hide this part of yourself because you've never felt that before." On the other hand, my parents were very comfortable with me liking the things I liked.

But I would tell them, "It's because these boys would tease me for this, and they will make fun of me."

So, most of the time, I had to interact with people who would tease me for the things that I liked or the way that I presented if I talked with a very high voice. Growing up, I had a very high voice, and I liked songs by Taylor Swift or Hannah Montana at that age. Musical theater was one of my main interests. Kids would bully me for that. So, I felt like I had to put up a front and pretend to be exactly like them. Nevertheless, the bullying continued, and teachers would never say anything or step in, [even though] we had a zero-tolerance policy for bullying. Obviously, it didn't feel good and made me feel ashamed for liking these things because I didn't feel justified.

This second frame of reference points to the human need to explore the concept of resilience.

What Is Resilience?

One of the most important aspects of empowerment is our capacity to acknowledge challenges and address them in ways that support us to see and celebrate our capacities to cope (Zacarian & Silverstone, 2020). Think of the herculean steps taken by students, families, schools, and local communities during COVID-19. We needed to be flexible, make adaptations, and draw from our strengths and capacities to cope with the prolonged stress that came with a virus unlike any we'd experienced in our lifetime. Resilience is our capacity to face challenges and recover from them by using our internal strengths (qualities we possess either inherently or have developed in response to stressful experiences). It also includes another vital condition, our capacity to be flexible and make the adaptations needed to flourish. A third element of resilience, which is not always present or included in this definition, is the capacity to contribute to support others in coping with challenges. We might call this courageous resilience on behalf of others.

Courageous Resilience on Behalf of Others

Sameer attended a private high school after his elementary and middle school years. In Chapter 4, we learned that Sameer's gender identity was accepted during his high school years. While there, he did more than advocate for himself. He courageously went back to his prior schools to support them in learning how to advocate for and support gay students. He also did a lot more.

Shining a Light on Empowerment Development
Leading to Resilience

I felt like I wanted to do something. Because I had been very lucky to find this queer community in high school and have supportive parents, I shouldn't have to be lucky to be able to come out and be supported. I wanted to do something to make schools safer and more inclusive. So, I returned to my old middle school and met with the principal and school counselor. I described all the bullying and what I went through. I told them that I believed the adults could have done a lot more to support me. And they listened. I was able to get a GSA (Gender-Sexuality Alliance club) started there. I helped train the teachers about gender identity and sexuality and teach the students antibullying lessons where we specifically emphasized that homophobic bullying is not okay. We made sure students knew ways to stand up for themselves or their friends. It was really empowering to make that kind of change in an environment where I'd been bullied so much.

At 16, during my junior year in high school, I started a nonprofit organization called Empathy Alliance (theempathyalliance.org). I also wrote a teacher's guide called *Read This, Save Lives* (Jha, 2018). I combined my story and things I've learned with tips for educators and data from studies and resources.

Now that I am in college, I shifted my focus to advocacy work. I've been working with the White House on how they can institute policies and legislation to make schools safe for trans youth. There is so much hateful rhetoric on the news. I'm working to address those on a policy level.

Figure 6.3. Continuum of Empowerment Development

Reprinted from Zacarian and Silverstone (2020), p. 130.

As humans, we have the capacity to develop new ways of thinking, act-ing, and reacting (Floyd & McKenna, 2003; Lerner et al., 2005; Zacarian & Silverstone, 2020). As you read Sameer's recollection from 2nd grade through high school years, consider the continuum of empowerment seen in Figure 6.3.

Students need to develop the skills of empowerment and feel iden-tity safe, with a sense of belonging, value, and competence in using these skills. Figures 6.1 and 6.2 provide us with the terms, words, idioms, and phrases (what Debbie calls TWIPs) associated with the skills of empower-ment. Educators and parents should see the development of empower-ment as a recursive process of learning, practicing, and reflecting on what we have learned to enact these empowerment skills fluidly. Drawing from the California English Language Development Standards (2012); New York State Department of Education (August 2022); and Haynes and Zacarian (2010), we describe these five levels of empowerment development to sup-port educators and parents to teach children these skills in Figure 6.4.

TAKING ACTION

One of the most powerful supports that Sameer has is his family. They sup-ported his playing with dolls and engaging in activities more frequently identified as ones associated with girls. Imagine how much Sameer's family might have done to advocate for his education and partner with his teachers had they known he was bullied! The type of partnership we are referring to was highlighted in the opening of this chapter, where we recounted the steps that Matthew's mother, Rebecca, took to support her son's participa-tion in class. She partnered with his teacher. When Matthew went to middle school, his parents learned that he did not have the skills needed to open his locker, an activity that middle schoolers routinely engage in. They learned of this challenge when Matthew shared what happened. As you read his mother's recounting of the experience, consider the steps that she and his school took to support Matthew to have a lock like his peers and engage in the same locking and unlocking routines as they do. Pay particular attention to what Rebecca says about the importance of "the little things."

Figure 6.4. Five Levels of Receptive and Assertive Empowerment

1. **Pre-emerging**: A student at this level is just beginning to learn the receptive and assertive terms, words, idioms, and phrases and is dependent on (1) listening carefully to their teacher for definitions, explanations, and demonstrations of the empowerment terminology in practice (e.g., what does it explicitly mean to observe carefully), (2) modeling what the actions mean and look like in a specific context by using visuals to support understanding (e.g., using sentence prompts for such terms as when I listen carefully, I look like . . . , I respond like . . . , I add to the conversation by . . .); and (3) multiple practice opportunities to begin to use the language of receptive and assertive empowerment after seeing models for these.

2. **Emerging**: A student at the emerging level is starting to use the receptive and assertive language of empowerment in reference to themselves and others in specific contexts. However, explicit instruction and modeling continue to be needed in order to support students at this level to practice using these skills in context (such as when socializing with others at recess, lunch, and after- or out of school, as well as in learning in the classroom)—using the language provided in Figures 6.1. and 6.2, a teacher responds to the receptive language that a student communicates. For example, the teacher says: Jackie, I appreciate how you are carefully listening to the opinions of your classmate and sharing your own thoughts, feelings, and ideas.

3. **Developing**: A student is beginning to demonstrate a small amount of autonomy in using the assertive and receptive skills of empowerment. A student's teacher(s) and/or family member(s) routinely acknowledge when the student demonstrates these skills. For example, using the language provided in Figures 6.1. and 6.2, a teacher responds to the receptive language that a student communicates. He says: Jackie, I appreciate how you are carefully listening to the opinions of your classmate and sharing your own thoughts, feelings, and ideas.

4. **Enacting**: A student is showing an increased level of autonomy and independence. The student is demonstrating (in body, spoken, and written language) appropriate usage of receptive and assertive empowerment communication across a wide swath of social and academic environments. While students have achieved this level of development, it is important for teachers and families to support them in using these skills on a routine basis. The example furnished earlier for the third stage is needed to be used for students in the fourth stage so that there is a continuous model for and acknowledgment of students' empowerment dialogue.

5. **Integrating**: A student at the integrating level communicates using the language of empowerment in the receptive *and* assertive realms and uses them readily in a variety of settings and contexts. Students at this level of proficiency continue to receive acknowledgment from their teacher for their empowerment efforts on behalf of themselves and others.

Reflection Task

Reflect on the Levels of Empowerment:

1. Return to the example furnished at the opening of this chapter. Assign Matthew a level of empowerment based on the five proficiency levels listed in Figure 6.3 and explained in Figure 6.4.
2. What evidence do you have to support the level you assigned?
3. Return to Sameer's reflection of himself during his high school and college years. Assign Sameer a level of empowerment based on the five proficiency levels assigned in Figure 6.3 and the subsequent explanation explained in Figure 6.4 of these levels.
4. What evidence do you have to support the level you assigned?
5. Select one of your students and describe their level of empowerment using the language from Figures 6.1, 6.2, 6.3, and 6.4.

As part of the transition to middle school, it is a rite of passage for students to finally have a real locker with a combination lock. However, for a student like Matthew, this can be anxiety provoking. Students have very little time between classes to unlock their locks and retrieve items from their lockers. Matthew had a really difficult time unlocking the lock to his locker and was often arriving at class with the wrong books or without books because he could not open his locker and was embarrassed to ask for help or admit he could not do it. After school one day, Matthew told me about this situation. So, I emailed his guidance counselor, and we came up with a plan. Originally the guidance counselor suggested that we just remove the lock from his locker—but I did not want Matthew to have anything different than the rest of the students or to have any identifiable accommodations that might embarrass him or single him out differently. So instead, after some research, we learned that we could alter Matthew's lock to make it "unlockable" so that it could never truly lock—and so any combination would open the lock—but that it would still look the same to others. This prevented him from being embarrassed about not being able to open his locker at school.

Sometimes we can get so caught up in the big picture that we forget it is often the little things, like a lock on a locker, that can be the difference for a student to be able to attend class with a sense of confidence, safety, and value.

Reflection Task

Reflect on How to Support the Empowerment of Your Students:

1. Return to Sameer's reflection about his parents and the steps they took
   to support his emerging nonbinary identity. Also, return to Rebecca's
   description of supporting her son, Matthew, to feel that he is a member
   of his class by engaging in the common ordinary task of opening his
   locker. Discuss the steps that their parents took to support their child.
2. What might you do to support students such as Sameer and Matthew to
   feel safe, that they are members of your classroom or school community,
   valued, and competent?

EMPOWERING STUDENTS' IDENTITIES AS LEARNERS

In Chapter 4, we shared how *student-centered teaching* emerged in the SISP
study as an important domain for promoting identity safety and contributing to a robust academic identity. That domain includes four components:
listening for student voices, focus on cooperation, teaching for understanding, and
classroom autonomy. Using the empowerment continuum, we can incorporate
opportunities for students to develop and use their voices, learn valuable
collaboration skills, develop increasing levels of autonomy, and take charge of
their learning.

Additional goals for reaching the enacted and integrated levels of empowerment are to

- fortify children's understanding of the roots of negative judgments
  by others; and
- support them to draw from these understandings to counter
  negative stereotypes and embrace an unhampered sense of agency
  and potential for academic and social growth.

For Matthew, when his teacher, guidance counselor, and parents paid
careful attention to what motivated him and took steps to ensure he felt included, his sense of identity safety was strengthened. In addition, he felt an
increased belonging and engagement with school. For Sameer, a welcoming environment in high school empowered him to embrace his LGBTQ+
identity, speak with his parents more openly about his identity, and become a leader. As an empowered student at the age of 15, he achieved the
integrating stage of empowerment development. A demonstration of this
level of development is the letter that Sameer wrote to the Pope that was

featured in a Huffington Post article entitled "Dear Pope, Don't Transgender Children Need Your Love Too?" (Jha, 2016).

Throughout the book, we have described instances where stereotype threat and implicit and explicit bias can diminish a child's sense of academic prowess and beliefs about their intelligence through negative stereotypes about their race, knowledge of the English language, gender, and other experiences. In addition to creating warm and identity safe spaces, young people need specific guidance to enable them to face these obstacles. An example is the important conversation that Laura, a White woman, and her husband, who is African American, whom we met in Chapter 5 had with their older son. When he was 12, they discussed with him the type of brutality that he might experience in the future as a Black man and what to do when it happens.

> Ken, my husband, talked about his experiences in a generalized way, and then we showed our son what to do with his hands and what to say, explained why he should not run away, and described all of the physical things to do to keep himself as safe as possible.

PARTNERSHIPS BETWEEN HOME AND SCHOOL

Family and school environments provide invaluable opportunities for students to develop and strengthen their empowerment efforts. The same holds true for every environment in which students interact. The home-school partnership ideas we have included in each chapter help us envision the possibilities of working with and on behalf of students so that they can enact and continuously practice their pre-emerging, emerging, developing, enacting, and integrating skills of empowerment. Most importantly, these environments should provide a safe space for students to

- gain a deeper understanding of and appreciation for who they are, what they can contribute, and why these skills of empowerment matter; and
- find value in, acknowledge, and celebrate how they cope with challenges.

There are many activities that schools and individual teachers can create to support family-school partnerships. Here are several ideas adapted from Zacarian and Silverstone (2015, 2020).

Examples of Home-School Partnerships With Children's Involvement

- **Routinely share what students are doing well in school**. Parents/guardians and educators can celebrate successes large and small. As described in Chapter 2, find out a parent's/guardian's language needs and preference for communication (e.g., text, email, phone calls).
- **Hold student-led conferences** where students are empowered to share their learning with their families and teacher. These can occur in the school, synchronically, and using computer-mediated formats where parents might see a video recording, Google doc, or other means (Zacarian & Silverstone, 2020). Helpful strategies for doing this in K–12 include
  - » brainstorm meeting times for the student and their family and indicate if the student-led conference will be held in-person or online;
  - » prepare students to be empowered by supporting them in creating a portfolio of their work, planning what they would like to share during the meeting, and preparing responses to questions parents-/guardians-families are likely to ask;
  - » cowrite an invitation with students; and
  - » at the conference, support students to reflect on what is going well by having them respond to the following sentence stems:
    - Things that are going well in [subject] class include . . .
    - When I feel the strongest as a learner, I am . . .
    - A challenge that I am having includes. . . . I am addressing it by . . .
    - A sample of my classwork is. . . . I think it is a fine example of . . .
    - Celebrate the student-led conference and make plans for future ones.
- **Co-plan and enact social events with students**, such as potluck suppers or tea or dance parties. These activities should involve students as co-planners with us. They know their parents and guardians much better than we do, and they also know us much better than their parents and guardians do!
  - » Support students in the various phases of the events, such as who will greet parents/guardians at the door, where they will sit, what type of food and space is needed, and more.
  - » Invite students to find ways to share authentic aspects of their multidiverse identities.

　　　» Cowrite invitations with students and build momentum for the
　　　　event by sending reminders through various channels, including
　　　　a school's website, video chat reminders created by students
　　　　(as well as multilingual translators as needed), and using other
　　　　creative means to boost parent/guardian attendance.
　　　» Have students welcome families, support families during the
　　　　event, and hold a closing activity.
　• **Co-plan and enact events for students to demonstrate their
　　learning**. Empower students to create and enact events such as
　　science fairs, debates, and poetry slams that demonstrate their
　　academic learning by using the same strategies listed in co-planning
　　social events. Keep in mind that students of all ages and grade
　　levels love to participate in planning a program, like reading stories
　　they have written aloud to share with parents/guardians.
　• **Co-build a home-school culture of learning.** We want every
　　family to be our partner. It is helpful to hold family curriculum
　　events where families and children engage in activities such as
　　a mathematics game night, writer's workshop, story-sharing,
　　chemistry demonstration, or college application process meeting.
　　Events such as a game night to support children and families to
　　engage in multiplication activities and science experiments at home
　　can be a fine way to make learning transparent. Again, rather than
　　plan this meeting on our own, enlist students' support in creating
　　the event for them and their families. Use the same strategies as
　　are listed for social events. The intent of these events is for families
　　to take the ideas they learn home and interact with their children
　　about them. As with social events, they are also an opportunity for
　　students and families to gather and socialize together.

A Parent's Perspective on Supporting Students on the Autism Spectrum

We understand that each child has a unique personality, sensory-motor
needs, and qualities. While this is important to understand, Rebecca offers
some helpful insights for supporting students on the autism spectrum. Here
are Rebecca's responses to questions that we asked.

　*How can schools best serve the academic needs of children on the autism
　　spectrum?*
　I would say listening is one of the most essential skills a teacher can
　have when it comes to supporting kids with ASD (autism spectrum

disorder). Parents often know best what rewards, motivates, and challenges their children. Teachers should look for ways to facilitate open communication with their students' families via email, text, or a monthly check-in *outside* the routine IEP or parent-teacher conferences. Close communication with my son's team (OT, PT, Speech, Academic, Guidance, and Special Ed liaison) is really what has kept my child supported—by having opportunities to share ideas, feedback, or just likes/dislikes for my son because they change and evolve over the year.

What effective ways do you think educators should know about teaching children social skills and encouraging parents to do the same?

Teachers should know that it's important to teach healthy social strategies to everyone in the classroom, not just the ASD child. Provide ways to teach various social skills to all students. Each child thrives differently, spectrum or otherwise, so teaching to the entire class benefits the harmony of the classroom and the ASD student.

What strategies best support children to plan, focus their attention, remember instructions, and juggle multiple tasks successfully?

For my son, a visual daily planner works well. A chart shows the day's routine in chronological order, so they can visually see what to expect. Velcro is helpful, so if things change, they can be reordered easily. As my son got older, this became a daily planner, which he now uses to stay on top of homework and longer-term assignments. Also, don't put everything only on a screen or in a google classroom. It's important for students not always to have to rely on a screen to access their work. A screen at home is often a trap for easily distractible students. So, while they might have good intentions opening their laptop to access an assignment, it also creates a temptation to game, watch videos, etc., and parents can't always supervise every child during homework time if they are in their room, etc. This also helps to offer some variety over the week of how homework should be completed. Some can be online, but my son also brings home printed maps that need to be color-coded for social studies, science scavenger hunts (e.g., list 10 things in your home that use energy, etc.), or an assignment to go outside and chart the moon phases for the month. . . . Variety is important to give all learners an opportunity to succeed—not just screen learners.

Some adaptations can help with academic instruction—rereading questions out loud, additional test time, front-row seating for students that are easily distractible, and opportunities for motor breaks. For example, my son had a 3rd-grade teacher that did yoga and breathing exercises in the room right after lunch every day to recenter and re-energize them for the afternoon.

What support helps children feel a sense of belonging and inclusion at school?

This is a really hard one because each child is different in what provides them a sense of belonging. I would say variety here is most important. Not all kids will do well with rapid-fire questions, classroom discussions, show and tell, etc., so look for ways to support children to engage in the classroom in a variety of ways. If you have a group assignment, mix it up—do some with student-organized groups and another with teacher-assigned groups.

It's also important to recognize that the times when ASD students struggle the most socially are when teachers are not there (recess, lunch, bus, etc.). So, look for opportunities to educate others (recess supervisors, bus drivers, cafeteria crew, etc.) of things that you know might either trigger or support your ASD student so that they can thrive in these environments (e.g., if your ASD student thrives on repetitive routine, they might benefit from having the same seat on the bus every day; otherwise, it could start their day off already feeling anxious. If you know this about them, share this insight with the bus staff or driver).

What home-school partnerships do you feel are or have been the most beneficial?

In addition to the things listed above, having an open line of communication is most important. A parent should NEVER be surprised at a parent-teacher conference—because if something is going on, a teacher or parent should create the opportunity to communicate about it as it is happening versus waiting. Much like in the real world, a good manager gives feedback along the way and does not wait for their employee's annual review.

Positively Countering Opposition

Some critics claim that teaching about LGBTQ+ people is tantamount to a "gay agenda" that seeks to turn children gay. They add that it is inappropriate for young children because they are too young to learn about sex. They are misinformed. Vinnie, whom we met in Chapter 1, explains,

I think people misconstrue or misinterpret that learning about lesbian, gay, bisexual, transgender, nonbinary people represents teaching something sexually explicit. A child learning that a student has two mommies is no different from knowing that a child has a mommy and a daddy.

In his Huffington Post article, Sameer (Jha, 2016) wrote,

> In my current private school, we have not yet had sex ed or biology (it's taught in 11th grade), but the teachers are accepting and willing to accommodate every student. They will use the pronouns the student asks them to [use]. In English class, our teacher stressed the fact that they/them pronouns are completely valid and grammatically correct third-person singular pronouns. The teachers are not "converting" people, just accepting them for who they already are.

In both examples, acknowledging and validating the existence of LGBTQ+ people have nothing to do with sex. Throughout history and in all cultures worldwide, a portion of the population has always been LGBTQ+. Often, as we have seen, young children like Vinnie or Sameer are bullied and ostracized for not fitting into gender norms, even before hearing the word "gay." Vinnie and Sameer had to overcome years of disempowerment before they could be fully empowered to embrace their identities. Meanwhile, Tris, a nonbinary college student who uses they/them pronouns, shared

> I was raised with a lot of "girl power" messaging. So, I felt a lot of pride in being a girl. Then, in 7th or 8th grade, I already knew I liked girls and boys. It's funny because I don't remember how I came to the realization. I remember that at some point, I realized I'm nonbinary or gender fluid. I recalled feelings of gender dysphoria when I was younger. So, over the summer, before I went to high school, I changed my name and started introducing myself with my new name, my current name. And then, I legally changed it during my sophomore year of high school. Getting my parents to use my name was not a problem but getting them to remember always to use my pronouns has been a process. Since then, my gender identity hasn't changed.

For Tris, the growing awareness of their gender identity and the support of their parents and the school community has been empowering. Identity safety aims to raise awareness and acceptance for children and families along all points of the expansive gender spectrum.

Supporting Parent/Guardian Empowerment Fosters Their Sense of Identity Safety

When we work to empower parents/guardians, we are creating an identity safe space for them which has multiple benefits (Cohn-Vargas et al., 2022). We draw on their strengths and assets, validating them, and in turn, they become identity safe role models for their children. It also builds the caring school community we spoke of in Chapter 2. We can do this by

- giving parents roles in school governance and problem-solving,
- offering meaningful participation, including identifying areas that need improvement and advising on school decisions, and
- identifying needs academically and socially and helping the school provide resources that help families.

In Chapter 3, we discussed the power of Working Groups that shift the leadership dynamics from a hierarchy to a culture of collaboration. We can enhance involvement by working with community groups that represent the cultures and backgrounds of the school and neighborhood. During the height of the COVID-19 pandemic, in the Brockton District in Massachusetts, teams of bilingual-bicultural parent/guardian volunteers, paraprofessionals, counselors, and nurses staffed a multilingual call center, providing support and access to desperately needed medical, counseling, and food services for families, staff, and students as it was one of the most COVID-19 impacted cities in the state (Zacarian & Cohn-Vargas, 2020). The Brockton Public Schools and its community partners are great examples of identity safe practices being enacted.

Authors Debbie and Becki have worked with schools across the country. Here are a few examples of the ways schools have creatively involved the community in bringing needed resources to families:

- Weekly farmers markets bringing locally grown healthy food to campus, with students helping to distribute the food
- Volunteer dentists providing dental care to students
- County mental health workers providing on-site counseling services to students and families
- Employment workshops for parents/guardians about resume writing, interviewing, as well as finding employment and training programs.
- Former gang members providing small groups for teens on how they changed their lives.
- Groups for toddlers and parents/guardians for early learning activities

These activities serve to fulfill the many needs of families. In addition, they create a sense of belonging for families, modeling community resilience and unity.

LOOKING AHEAD

In this chapter, we explored the foundational principles and practices for supporting students' empowerment, agency, and resilience. Our final chapter examines how we can integrate and apply all identity safe practices we presented throughout the chapters and support them through engaging in continuous professional growth.

ADDITIONAL RESOURCES

- **Starting a Gender & Sexualities Alliance [GSA]**
  GSA Network. (n.d.). 10 steps for starting a GSA. https://gsanetwork.org /resources/10-steps-for-starting-a-gsa/
- **Supporting Students' Self-Advocacy**
  Zacarian, D., & Silverstone, M. A. (2020). *Teaching to empower: Taking action to foster student agency, self-confidence, and collaboration* (Chapter 7). ASCD.
- **Student Autonomy**
  Steele, D. M., & Cohn-Vargas, B. (2013). *Identity safe classrooms, K–5: Places to belong and learn* (pp. 51–62). Corwin.
  Cohn-Vargas, B., Kahn, A. C., & Epstein, A. (2021). *Identity safe classrooms, grades 6–12: Pathways to belonging and learning* (pp. 105–118). Corwin.
- **Community Involvement to Support Students with Disabilities**
  Lusa, L. (2022, July 25). *Engaging community support to empower diverse families of students with disabilities.* Edutopia. https://www.edutopia .org/article/engaging-community-support-empower-diverse-families -students-disabilities/

CHAPTER 7

Moving Away From "Same Old Habits" to Professional Growth

> Emmanuel's kindergarten teacher was phenomenal. Then he went on to 1st grade. It was October. He'd been in school a month when his 1st-grade teacher sat me down and the first thing she said was, "Your son should have never left kindergarten. He doesn't know his ABCs and shouldn't even be here."
>
> Lenore, professor and mother of Emmanuel

As humans, we have all found ourselves in situations where our perceptions and assumptions are different from others'. Imagine how Lenore, whom we met in Chapter 4, felt as she heard what was being said about her son entering 1st grade. In these situations, we hope that we have the grace, presence of mind, agility, and good sense to provide an effective counterpoint that will support identity safety—especially when it comes to our most precious loved ones, our children. Ideally, identity safety is integrated amongst and between a child's school and home communities. The duality of our purpose is to support educators and families to use and infuse identity safe practices throughout a child's life and take full advantage of the possibilities that can be realized through a strengths-based lens. One of the most eloquent and prolific educational scholars is Lisa Delpit. She deftly recounts the brilliance of her daughter's imagination and poetry (2001) against the backdrop of the deficit labels that her child's teachers applied to her. It led to her arduous decision to move her child to a new school where her talents were celebrated. One of the most important aspects of our dual purpose is so that we, as educators and parents/guardians, can embrace an assets-based approach that involves copartnering with families by taking time to identify, honor, value, and work from children's assets and capacities. Like Lisa Delpit, Lenore chose a new school for her child. She explains how a strength-based approach—coupled with using strategies that were specifically designed to support her son to learn—made all the difference.

Now, in 6th grade, he's getting a lot of support. They set time aside every day to work on his homework. A special educator works with him, and the school corresponds with parents every week. We know what the homework assignments are. In fact, if there is any concern, I already receive an email before I pick him up from school. He's been on the honor roll for the last 3 months of marking periods. His report card came back with three Bs and three As. I think he feels like he's part of a community in a space where he belongs.

Adaptations, such as listening to audiobooks and converting voice-to-text, greatly supported Emmanuel to be successful in school and to draw from the strengths that he possessed inherently or as a result of the supports he received in elementary school. Additionally, he felt less othered and different by being in a school with students and staff who shared his racial identity. One of the greatest benefits that he has realized is a sense of identity safety and accomplishment. An example is a recent trip that Emmanuel and Lenore took to tour Historically Black Colleges and Universities (HBCUs). Emmanuel is now excitedly talking about the possibility of attending Morgan State or another HBCU. The shift from Emmanuel seeing himself as a struggling learner to a successful learner happened for many reasons, including the partnership that he, his mother, and his teachers have codeveloped.

In this chapter, we gather some of the big ideas and key takeaways from previous chapters as we explore:

- the changing role that educators can enact: moving away from the "same old habits";
- supporting identity safe practices at home;
- engaging in a cycle of inquiry; and
- professional growth tools for evaluating, strengthening, and celebrating home-school partnerships.

THE CHANGING ROLE THAT EDUCATORS CAN ENACT: MOVING AWAY FROM THE "SAME OLD HABITS"

In the opening of our chapter, Lenore describes her recollection of a parent-teacher conference. She stated, "I could not understand what she [the kindergarten teacher] was saying. It was so contrary to my experience of who he was." The importance of family engagement cannot be understated. We have years of research affirming the importance of building these positive human connections on behalf of students' success in school and beyond (Epstein et al., 2019; Espinosa, 2015; Robles de Meléndez & Beck, 2019). While we know its relevance, many of us continue to regard traditional activities such as the ritual of the parent-teacher conference as the time to share what is going well and what isn't.

MOVING FROM A STRENGTHS-WEAKNESSES BINARY TO A STRENGTHS-BASED STANCE

Using a strengths/weakness, good/bad, doing well/not doing well binary (though perhaps well-intentioned amongst the most seasoned of us) overlooks the positive possibilities of using an assets-based approach in all we do with students, their families, our school, and local communities, and, of course, ourselves. The example we furnished in the opening of this chapter reflects that strengths/weakness binary to an intense degree. Additionally, it did more than diminish the possibilities of a partnership; in the most basic of terms, it did great damage. Lenore's reflection about an IEP meeting that was held during her son's elementary years describes the school's misperception of Emmanuel's capacity as a learner.

> At the meeting, the IEP, the person who did the assessment told me that my son has deep dyslexia, and they were not sure if he would ever read above a 2nd-grade level.

Years later, Emmanuel attended a school that employed a strength-based stance coupled with a strong school-parent partnership approach. This paradigm swiftly shifts away from a strengths-weakness binary and takes advantage of a strengths-based, culturally responsive approach that makes great use of determining:

- what is going well,
- what needs strengthening, and
- how these strengthening actions can be made in partnership with families.

For this approach to work successfully, it requires an "all-in" school-based effort where everyone is focused on it working.

A hypothetical example of the "old" method in action is a deficits-based declaration from a paraprofessional about a student diagnosed with ADHD. The paraprofessional declares: "Oh, I work with that student. Her teacher told me not to expect any growth from her." What assumptions might you make about the paraprofessional's work with the student? There are countless examples, like this one, that exemplify our strengths/weaknesses binary. Our point in illustrating some of them in a chapter devoted to putting the pieces of our book together is to show how powerful it can be when we enact identity safety with fidelity and when we don't.

The steps that we need to take are somewhat like two people with the same infection being prescribed medicine that requires each to take two pills every four hours. The first person takes the medication and feels better within 10 days. The second person opens the medicine bottle, takes one pill every day (1/10th of the total!), and returns to the doctor feeling even worse than he did before beginning the medicine regime. The doctor asks him how it went taking the medicine. "Oh, I tried!" he declares. Moving from a strengths/weakness to a strength-based stance takes a fair amount of intention, professionalism, and growth to make it a fully operationalized approach. Drawing from our example, the doctor kindly asks her patient if he was able to take eight pills a day. Reluctantly, he tells her that he only took one per day as he is afraid to take medicine. Together, they come up with a copowered solution that considers the patient's fears without being judgmental and includes the doctor's office checking on him to ensure that he is comfortable taking all of the medicine as prescribed. Throughout, the patient is praised for his efforts.

In the Introduction of our book, we discussed the urgency for children to hear, see, and experience the positives of synchronized, integrated, and interdependent identity safety in school and at home. We also shared the benefits of using a strength-based approach that supports a child's identity by highlighting their multidiverse personal, social, cultural, and academic strengths. Throughout the book, we have shown how our stance reflects changing trends in education from a strengths/weaknesses binary to a strengths-based stance where students' academic and social–emotional outcomes are enhanced when we copartner with families.

Rethinking the strengths of our identity safe partnerships calls for us to engage in a self- and collective evaluation of our policies, practices, and structures. Additionally, it calls for providing professional growth in areas that we find need strengthening. For example, as we discussed in earlier chapters, while many of us believe in the idea of working with families, too few of us have been formally trained to work with a multidiverse populace. In this chapter, we share ways to copartner, draw from previous chapters in our book, and provide tools for enacting identity safe partnership practices with families and local community members, agencies, and organizations. Here are some questions intended to help us begin looking more deeply at our partnership schema.

1. What role can educators play in strengthening our identity safe partnerships with families?
2. What are key considerations for engaging in these strengthening actions in an empowering way?
3. What tools should we use to evaluate the strengths of our identity safe practices and what needs strengthening?

These questions are important to consider. However, we don't want to begin our evaluation of our strengths-based and improvement plans by repeating what we have done in the past or using a simple checklist that requires yes/no responses. We must first move toward creating a collective of ideas, hopes, dreams, and areas that need strengthening to fully engage in partnership practices.

SUPPORTING IDENTITY SAFE PRACTICES AT HOME

One of the most action-oriented steps an educator can take is to support students for who they are and the tremendous assets that they possess. In the first and second chapters of our book, we discussed the importance of a welcoming and supportive environment where each child's identity is valued as a contributing member of their community. The same holds true for what we hope occurs at home so that children feel a sense of identity safety. One means for encouraging these practices at home is to share the many positives that we observe in school and support families in helping these to occur at home. Here are some examples taken from three strategies and suggestions that we offer in our first chapter:

1. *Give children rich positive experiences that continuously affirm their multiple and varied identities.*
    For example, share positive experiences that you have observed and had with their child, such as: "Abdul is a careful listener with his class partners. He takes time to clarify what he has heard and affirms what classmates have stated. I appreciate his collaborative leadership. Abdul is also a wonderful illustrator. Often when he works with a group, he draws what is being shared. His classmates and I appreciate his ability to visualize the key ideas. I appreciate what you are doing at home and welcome learning more about what you are doing. Please share the activities you engage in at home to support Abdul's strengths. I am excited to learn from you!"

2. *Support awareness and offer tools to deconstruct, dismantle, and counteract the power of the negative stereotypes about identity.*
    For example, share positive experiences you have observed and had with a child, such as: "Jamille is very strong at seeing when things are not fair in our class. For example, she noticed a classmate wasn't participating in a small group discussion. I appreciated her noticing this, sharing this with a group in a very polite and respectful way, and asking the small group to encourage their peer to speak. She is a natural mediator who seeks and encourages everyone's active participation! What activities do you do at home that support Jamille's leadership and empathy?"
3. *Help children come to celebrate different social identities and cultivate diversity as a rich shared resource.*
    For example, it is helpful to learn about the various personal, social, cultural, and life experiences of students and their families. We can do this by asking questions about children's strengths and assets. Our overall goal should be to learn about each child's and family's rich identities to support them to feel safe, have a sense of belonging, value, competence, and, as importantly, the confidence to share their thoughts, hopes, dreams, questions, and more in partnering with us. That stance involves our having a sense of curiosity to learn as much as we can about our students and their families. An application is asking students and families about the activities that they enjoy doing together and drawing from these to build affirmational partnerships. Let's say, for example, that we learn that a favorite activity of one family is taking the train to visit relatives in a nearby city. We learn that the child's father and uncle are professional jazz musicians, and that family often goes to their jazz performances. We ask the child if his father and uncle might like to come to our history class when we are studying the Jazz Age.

ENGAGING IN A CYCLE OF INQUIRY

An essential means for cultivating a shared understanding of identity safety is a cycle of inquiry, as seen in Figure 7.1. It is intended to be used by individuals and groups.

The cycle of inquiry is not intended to occur all at once or at a particular pace. Rather, its purpose is to guide and sustain authentic partnerships

Figure 7.1. Cycle of Inquiry

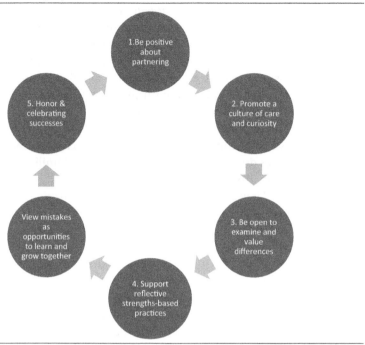

between and amongst students, families, staff, and collaborative groups. With this as our shared goal, here are some general guidelines for each element within the cycle.

1. **Be Positive About Partnering**
   - » Create a welcoming school environment. Get to know all students, staff, and parents/guardians. Continuously communicate the value of partnerships.
   - » Create opportunities for collaboration and practice sharing ideas and learning from one another.
   - » Create teams with diverse members. Build trust and ensure that all voices are heard. Welcome people to express their authentic identities and varied points of view and work toward common goals to benefit everyone.

2. **Promote a Culture of Care and Curiosity**
   - » Create opportunities for everyone to get to know each other in nonjudgmental ways and to learn about their hopes, dreams, challenges, and needs.

» Build a culture of innovation where new ideas and solutions are welcome.

3. **Be Open to Examine and Value Differences**

    » Communicate the value of diversity and encourage them to share differences. When children have different identities (e.g., gender identities and disabilities) than their parents/guardians, help build understanding.

    » Model the willingness to share some of your differences. Create spaces where different perspectives are welcomed.

    » Notice how people like to express themselves and avoid putting people on the spot.

4. **Support Reflective Strengths-Based Practices**

    » Observe student strengths and recognize each child's unique qualities. Even when a child is struggling, look deeper to find their strengths. Regularly communicate those strengths to families in person, through progress reports, and other forms of communication.

    » Create a culture of strength-based learning and share best practices.

    » Communicate the value of a strength-based approach and draw on the strengths of team members.

5. **View Mistakes as Opportunities to Learn and Grow Together**

    » Teach everyone that mistakes and failures happen to all of us and are opportunities for learning and growing together.

    » Create a nonjudgmental culture where people feel safe to share times they have failed and what they learned.

    » Take responsibility for your mistakes. Model for the group that learning from mistakes and failures offers a chance to grow. Help everyone learn how to do it.

6. **Honor and Celebrate Successes**

    » Communicate incremental progress. Help students, parents/educators, and staff learn to celebrate successes—express enthusiasm about each child's potential in the context of high expectations.

    » Engage in patterns of regularly celebrating individual progress.

    » Create a feeling of collaboration by highlighting group accomplishments.

Reflection Task

Consider the possibilities of a Working Group in your professional context. Describe how this cycle of inquiry will support

1. partnering with multidiverse families, and
2. the mission and goals work of your Working Group.

TOOLS FOR ENGAGING FAMILIES

Family surveys, such as Resource 7.1 (on p. 142), are useful tools for identifying meaningful activities for students and families. One example is a group of Ukrainian newcomers who fled the war raging in their homeland. Rather than assume what these families and their children need, a survey can be an excellent tool for them to share what they hope, desire, and need for their children to succeed. A second example is a group of young students interested in creating a school garden to support the lack of fresh fruits and vegetables available to their community. A family survey can greatly help us enlist families for their expertise (e.g., carpenters and gardeners) in this student-led effort. A third example is a group of families interested in creating after-school clubs to support their children's budding career interests. Resource 7.1 can provide Working Groups with helpful information about the types of activities that will yield the most meaningful action because it is based on actual up-to-date information from families.

Resource 7.1, adapted from Zacarian et al. (2021), is intended to help us support students' health and well-being and participation in after- and out-of-school activities. It should be translated into the different languages spoken by families in your school community.

PARTNERING WITH THE LARGER COMMUNITY

Once we know the desires and needs of families in our community, we can identify members of the larger community who can assist us. Working Groups can organize and facilitate these efforts in ways that no one person could ever accomplish on their own. They can also help in securing a partner that believes in the same strengths-based ideology as we strive to use. An example is Wolfe Street Academy in Baltimore, Maryland. They work in close partnership with the University of Maryland School of Dentistry to respond to students' dental needs (Vargas, 2016; Zacarian et al., 2017). There are three considerations for engaging in meaningful school-community partnerships.

1. *Recruit individuals and associations/organizations who believe in a strengths-based ideology.*
2. *Continuously analyze the changing needs of students to identify what is working and what needs strengthening.* For example, at Wolfe Street Academy, the needs of children changed as they began to routinely receive dental care. Accordingly, their partnership with the University of Maryland transformed to preventative nutritional, oral health, and hygiene care.
3. *Look for ways that everyone can be copowered so it is a mutually beneficial relationship instead of a hierarchical one.* For example, interns from the University of Maryland's Dental School receive invaluable experience, and Wolfe Street Academy's students and families are copowered in supporting the school's dental health and well-being (Zacarian et al., 2017; Zacarian et al., 2021).

These three considerations can be reinforced using the cycle of inquiry in Figure 7.1 and family survey in Resource 7.1.

PROFESSIONAL GROWTH TOOLS FOR EVALUATING, STRENGTHENING, AND CELEBRATING HOME-SCHOOL PARTNERSHIPS

One of the most important ways to ensure identity safety is continuous professional growth as a system-wide effort. Our book provides the theoretical underpinnings about and practices for engaging in identity safety. We also furnish a wide swath of interview and contributor voices that bring the principles and practices to life. They share powerfully personal experiences to support our collective understanding about working with our ever-growing and changing student and family populations and society itself. While no one book could ever provide a complete picture of any one topic, we believe that the broad range of voices included in this book greatly helps us all understand the critical importance of identity safety. Indeed, despite our depth of scholarship on this topic, the power of the personal stories shared in this book has deepened our awareness and practice of identity safety. With this explanation, we close our book with three professional development tools (Resource 7.1, Figures 7.2. and 7.3). We include these for the purpose of revisiting each of the preceding chapters to:

- understand and promote identity safety on a deeper level,
- prevent, address, and eliminate negative experiences that undermine identity safety, and
- consider what is already in practice at your school and what can be added

Resource 7.1: Family Survey

The purpose of this survey is to help us support your child's health and well-being, and social interests and desires and build strong family-school partnerships. Your responses will greatly help us in these efforts. Thank you!

Please check the resource that you believe are most needed:

☐ Medical
☐ Dental
☐ Eye care
☐ Housing
☐ Nutritional
☐ Counseling/mental health and well-being
☐ Childcare
☐ Parent workshops on advocating for my child and supporting my child's learning
☐ Other [please list]

Please check three family-school partnership activities that you think would be most helpful to your child:

☐ Family gatherings for social purposes (for example, a potluck meal, multicultural celebration, family picnic, or school dance)
☐ Family gatherings for children to demonstrate their learning
☐ Sports
☐ Ways for families to share resources such as their careers, hobbies, interests, and cultural celebrations. We welcome family involvement! Some ideas might include the following and much more!
☐ Carpentry projects
☐ Gardening
☐ Science activities
☐ Cultural activities music: ___ art:_____ dance:____ cooking:____ other: ____
☐ Career activities
☐ Creating a shared home-school culture of learning (For example, a game night or activity that can be done at home to support students' learning).
☐ Other [please describe]

(continued)

Resource 7.1: Family Survey (*continued*)

What is the best method to contact you to support our partnership efforts?

Please check three activities that you believe would be most beneficial to your child:

☐ After-school clubs and recreational activities
☐ Before- and after-school programs
☐ Sports
☐ Field trips
☐ Buddy programs
☐ Other [please describe]

PROFESSIONAL GROWTH TOOL FOR IDENTIFYING WHAT IS OCCURRING AND WHAT TO ADD

Figure 7.2 offers a self-reflection checklist of activities that correspond with Chapters 1–6 in our book. It is intended to be used as a guide for determining

1. what is already occurring and what it looks like in practices *and/or*
2. what will occur so that it will be added to our professional practice.

This tool is intended for teachers, coaches, supportive supervisors, as well as for book study and determining the professional development activities that are needed to strengthen our collective practice as a school or district community, grade level or subject matter group and others who wish to strengthen practice.

Figure 7.2. Self-Reflection Activities

	What I already do and what it looks like in my practice.	What I will add to my professional practice and how it will look.
Chapter 1		
Instilling pride in a child's identity		
Teaching children to embrace diversity		
Providing opportunities for students to be with others who share their identities		
Bolstering identity using a strength-based stance		
Chapter 2		
Creating a caring, trusting, and compassionate school culture		
Knowing our students and listening to them		
Moving from a deficit-based to asset-based growth mindset		
Chapter 3		
Reflecting on our identities, values, and implicit and explicit biases		
Considering trauma and influences of adverse experiences and racial trauma		
Recognizing differences between our experience and our students'		
Sharing our vulnerabilities and building a mistake-safe culture		
Chapter 4		
Supporting positive identity development for multidiverse children including racial/ethnic, gender, multilingual and academic student identities		
Understanding some unique aspects of identity: multiple heritages, intersectionality		
Using identity safety cues (ISCs)		
Countering homophobia, transphobia, racism, and other forms of bias and microaggressions		

(continued)

Figure 7.2. Self-Reflection Activities (*continued*)

	What I already do and what it looks like in my practice.	What I will add to my professional practice and how it will look.
Chapter 5		
Promoting cooperation and compassion		
Reducing prejudice and bias		
Cultivating self-awareness, self-regulation, and self-compassion to strengthen positive relationships		
Fostering a culturally inclusive growth mindset		
Helping children learn to be allies and upstanders who stand up for themselves and others		
Reducing and addressing implicit biases		
Chapter 6		
Empowering agency in children through receptiveness and assertiveness		
Supporting children in becoming resilient		
Cultivating strong academic identities in students		

Partnership Schema

Throughout the book, we offer a schema for developing strong, inclusive, and empowered partnerships with parents/guardians. Like Figure 7.2, Figure 7.3 is a tool intended to support these efforts looking at what is occuring and/or what will occur.

Figure 7.3. Home-School Partnership Activities

Respond to each prompt (what I already do and what I will add).	
What I already do, what it looks like in my practice, and how it reflects what is written in the book (quote a sentence or two and cite page number).	What I will add to my professional practice, what it will look like, and how it will reflect what is written the book (quote a sentence or two and cite page number).
Noticing and listening to student and parent/guardian voices	
Introducing identity safety to students, staff, and parents/guardians	
Forming a Working Group	
Assessing needs and learning about families through surveys, listening tours, and relationship-building	
Facilitating conversations about multidiverse identities at home and school	
Shifting from hierarchical to cooperative relationships between educators and parents/ guardians	
Inviting parents to help us understand children's backgrounds and facilitating developmentally appropriate conversations about multidiversity	
Fostering partnerships where educators reflect on implicit biases and listen to parents (e.g., supporting parents in accepting their LGBTQ+ children)	
Supporting students with disabilities through home-school partnerships	
Empowering parents'/guardians' sense of identity safety	
Drawing from community resources to support families	

Positively Countering Opposition

In each chapter, we described some of the opposition that educators experience individually and at the school and district levels. Using Resource 7.2, describe an experience where you (and/or others with whom you work) encountered opposition to critical race theory and curriculum and activities to foster an appreciation of diversity. Provide ways that you countered or might counter the opposition. Use a quote and page number from the book to support your counter. Complete this tool individually or collectively for the purpose of developing ways to address opposition positively.

CLOSING THOUGHTS

Our book aims to bring identity safety to the forefront of home-school partnerships. Our intent is to awaken and reawaken the positive possibilities that emerge when educators and families work together using identity safe practices to support children to flourish in all aspects of their lives. We shared vital research demonstrating the effectiveness of using a strengths-based, culturally responsive approach for children to hear a synchronized message of identity safety at home and in school. Our book also presented a wide array of multidiverse voices who courageously shared their personal experiences in hopes of a better world for our children.

We strongly believe that the type of solidarity we are advocating has the potential to exponentially expand students' endless capacities and to interrupt inequities in ways large, small, and everlasting. Our aim is that this book breaks new ground about the power of home-school identity safe partnerships. As partners in an ever-changing society, we can enhance children's physical, psychological, cognitive, social, and emotional development by listening to, learning from, and copowering each other toward valuing and honoring each member of our rich and diverse society. Our hope is that *Identity Safe Spaces at Home and School* helps us illuminate a path forward, and there is no better time to do this than right now.

Resource 7.2: Positively Countering Opposition

Chapter 1: Countering claims that critical race theory is indoctrination by educating parents about culturally sustaining practices.	
Positive ways to counter opposition.	Citation and page # to support my professional practice in countering opposition.

Chapter 2: Using inclusive strategies in response to people who claim that discussing diversity is divisive.	
Positive ways to counter opposition.	Citation and page # to support my professional practice in countering opposition.

Chapter 3: Responding to an interaction(s) that undermines the identity safety of other multidiverse parents/guardians	
Positive ways to counter opposition.	Citation and page # to support my professional practice in countering opposition.

Chapter 4: Explaining why teaching difficult parts of history should not be prohibited, does not harm children, is important for democracy, and can be done responsively without being divisive.	
Positive ways to counter opposition.	Citation and page # to support my professional practice in countering opposition.

Chapter 5: Using research on the effectiveness of social and emotional learning (SEL) in response to people who oppose teaching it.	
Positive ways to counter opposition.	Citation and page # to support my professional practice in countering opposition.

Chapter 6: Explaining why teaching about LGBTQ+ people is not teaching about sex and does not turn children gay, and a positive and supportive environment empowers LGBTQ+ student identity safety.	
Positive ways to counter opposition.	Citation and page # to support my professional practice in countering opposition.

Additional critiques of and opposition to diversity and identity safety	
Positive ways to counter this opposition.	Citation and page # to support my professional practice in countering opposition.

ADDITIONAL RESOURCES

- **Partnerships with Families and the Community**
  Cohn-Vargas, B., Kahn, A. C., Epstein, A., & Gogolewski, K. (2022). *Belonging and inclusion in identity safe schools: A guide for educational leaders* (pp. 141–171). Corwin.
- **Building Classroom, School, and Community Partnerships**
  Zacarian, D., Calderón, M. E., & Gottlieb, M. (2021). *Beyond crises: Overcoming linguistic and cultural inequities in communities, schools, and classrooms.* Corwin.
- **Working with Students and Families Who Are Experiencing or Have Experienced Adversity**
  Zacarian, D., Alvarez-Ortiz, L., Haynes, J. (2017). *Teaching to strengths: Supporting students living with trauma, violence, and chronic stress.* ASCD.

References

Agar, M. (1995). *Language shock: Understanding the culture of conversation.* William Morrow.

Agar, M. (2006). Culture: Can you take it anywhere?: Invited lecture presented at the Gevirtz Graduate School of Education, University of California at Santa Barbara. *International Journal of Qualitative Methods, 5*(2), 1–16. https://doi.org/10.1177/160940690600500201

Allport, G. (1954/1958/1979). *The nature of prejudice.* Perseus Books.

Anderson, M. (2022, September 26). *How social-emotional learning became a frontline in the battle against CRT.* NPR. https://www.npr.org/2022/09/26/1124082878/how-social-emotional-learning-became-a-frontline-in-the-battle-against-crt

Banks, J. A. (1997). Multicultural education: Characteristics and goals. In J. A. Banks & C. A. M. Banks (Eds.), *Multicultural Education: Issues and perspectives* (3rd ed.; pp. 3–31). Allyn & Bacon.

Bay Waters, L. (2022). *Kaleidoscope eyes: On being White in a multiracial world and family.* Self-published.

Bellanca, J., & Brandt, R. (2010). *21st century skills: Rethinking how students learn.* Solution Tree Press.

Berenberg, B. R. (1946). *The churkendoose* (D. Cunningham, Illus.). Wonder Books.

Bernhardt, B. C., & Singer, T. (2012). The neural basis of empathy. *Annual Review of Neuroscience, 35,* 1–23. doi:10.1146/annual-neuro-062111-150536

Bethell, C. D., Davis, M. B., Gombojav, N., Stumbo, S., & Powers, K. (2017, October). *A national and across-state profile on adverse childhood experiences among children and possibilities to heal and thrive.* Johns Hopkins Bloomberg School of Public Health. http://www.cahmi.org/projects/adverse-childhood-experiences-aces/

Biden, J. (2022, June 23). *Statement by President Joe Biden on the 50th anniversary of Title IX* [White House Briefing Room Statements and Releases]. https://www.whitehouse.gov/briefing-room/statements-releases/2022/06/23/statement-by-president-joe-biden-on-the-50th-anniversary-of-title-ix/

Brown, J. (1969). Say it loud—I'm Black, I'm proud [song]. On *Say It Loud—I'm Black and I'm Proud.* King Records.

Calderón, M. E. (2007). *Teaching reading to English language learners grades 6–12: A framework for improving achievement in the content areas.* Corwin Press.

California State Board of Education. (2012, November). *California English language development standards: Kindergarten through grade 12*. https://www.cde .ca.gov/sp/el/er/documents/eldstndspublication14.pdf

CASEL. (n,d.). Collaborative for Academic, Social, and Emotional Learning. https://casel.org/

Centers for Disease Control and Prevention. (2021). *Fast fact: Preventing bullying*. https://www.cdc.gov/violenceprevention/youthviolence/bullyingresearch /fastfact.html

Cohen, D. K. (1988). *Teaching Practice: Plus ça change*. National Center for Research on Teacher Education.

Cohn-Vargas, B. (2007). *Nurturing identity safety in elementary classrooms: A participatory action research study of effective strategies that validate students' backgrounds and cultures while promoting academic and social success* [Unpublished doctoral dissertation]. Fielding Graduate University.

Cohn-Vargas, B., & Rabideaux, P. (2023, January). Identity, safety, belonging for Native American students: Becki Cohn-Vargas interviews Paula Rabideaux. *Language Magazine*.

Cohn-Vargas, B., & Steele, D. (2016). Creating identity safe classroom environments. *Illinois Reading Council Journal, 44*(3), 23–32.

Cohn-Vargas, B., Kahn, A. C., & Epstein, A. (2021). *Identity safe classrooms, grades 6–12: Pathways to belonging and learning*. Corwin.

Cohn-Vargas, B., Kahn, A. C., Epstein, A., & Gogolewski, K. (2022). *Belonging and inclusion in identity safe schools: A guide for educational leaders*. Corwin.

Comer, J. P. (2005). Childhood and adolescent development: The critical missing focus in school reform. *Phi Delta Kappan*. https://doi.org/10.1177 /003172170508601008

Cornish, A. (2022, November 17). Meet the parents taking over school boards [Audio podcast episode]. In *The Assignment with Audie Cornish*. CNN. https:// www.cnn.com/audio/podcasts/the-assignment/episodes/b590d874-12bb -4b45-bfae-af4d01024b0f

Costa, A. (2017). Foreword. In B. Kallick & A. Zmuda, *Students at the center: Personalized learning with habits of mind* (pp. ix–xi). ASCD.

Crenshaw, K. (2020). *On intersectionality: Essential writings*. The New Press.

C-SPAN. (2020, April 9). User Clip: Fauci: Coronavirus "is shining a bright light" on health disparities. https://www.c-span.org/video/?c4867412/user-clip -faucicoronavirus-is-shining-bright-light-health-disparities

Darling-Hammond, L. & Cook-Harvey, C. (September 7, 2018). *Educating the whole child: Improving school climate to support student success*. Learning Policy Institue. https://learningpolicyinstitute.org/product/educating-whole-child-report

DeCapua, A., & Marshall, H. W. (2010). Students with limited or interrupted formal education in US classrooms. *The Urban Review, 42*, 159–173.

Decker, S., & Mahal, M. (2014). *Define upstander*. Not in Our Town. https:// www.niot.org/blog/define-upstander

Delpit, L. (2001). "Skin deep" learning. In P. Rodis, A. Garrod, and M. L. Boscardin (Eds). *Learning disabilities and life stories* (pp. 157–164). Pearson.

Delpit, L. (2006). *Other people's children: Cultural conflict in the classroom*. New Press.

Derman-Sparks, L., & Ramsey, P. G. (2006). *What if all the kids are white? Anti-bias multicultural education with young children and families.* Teachers College Press.

Devine, P. G., Forscher, P. S., Austin. A. J., & Cox, W. L., (2012). Long-term reduction in implicit race bias: A prejudice habit-breaking intervention. *Journal of Experimental Social Psychology, 48*(6):1267–1278. https://doi:10.1016/j.jesp.2012.06.003

Dewey, J. (1938). *Experience and education.* Collier Books.

Durlak, J. A., Weissberg, R. P., Dymnicki, A. B., Taylor, R. D., & Schellinger, K. B. (2011). The impact of enhancing students' social and emotional learning: A meta-analysis of school-based universal interventions. *Child Development, 82*(1), 405–432. https://doi.org/10.1111/j.1467-8624.2010.01564.x

Dweck, C. S. (2006). *Mindset: The new psychology of success.* Random House.

Dweck, C., Walton, G. M., & Cohen, G. L. (2014). *Academic tenacity: Mindsets and skills that promote long-term learning.* Bill and Melinda Gates Foundation. https://ed.stanford.edu/sites/default/files/manual/dweck-walton-cohen-2014.pdf

Eberhardt, J., Purdie, V., Goff, P. A., & Davies, P. (2004). Seeing Black: Race, crime, and visual processing. *Journal of Personality and Social Psychology, 87*(6), 876–893.

Editors of Encyclopaedia Britannica. (n.d.). Critical race theory. In *Encyclopaedia Britannica.* Retrieved from https://www.britannica.com/topic/critical-race-theory

Epstein, J. L., Greenfield, M. D., Hutchins, D. J., Williams, K. J., & Sanders, M. G. (2019). *School, family, and community partnerships: Your handbook in action* (4th ed.). Corwin.

Espinosa, L. (2015). *Getting it right for young children from diverse backgrounds: Applying research to improve practice with a focus on dual language learners* (2nd ed.) Pearson.

Esseks, J. (2020, August 28). *Open letter to schools about LGBTQ student privacy.* American Civil Liberties Union. https://www.aclu.org/documents/open-letter-schools-about-lgbtq-student-privacy?redirect=letter/open-letter-schools-about-lgbt-student-privacy

Felitti, V. J., Anda, R. F., Nordenberg, D., Williamson, D. F., Spitz, A. M., Edwards, V., Koss, M. P., & Marks, J. S. (1998). Relationship of childhood abuse and household dysfunction to many of the leading causes of death in adults: The Adverse Childhood Experiences (ACE) study. *American Journal of Preventive Medicine, 14*(4), 245–258.

Floyd, D. T., & McKenna, L. (2003). National youth organization in the United States: Contributions to civil society. In D. Wertlieb, F. Jacobs, & R. M. Lerner (Eds.), *Handbook of applied developmental science: Promoting positive children, adolescent, and family development through research, policies and programs* (Vol. 3; pp. 11–26). Sage.

Fulbeck, K. (2006). *Part Asian, 100% Hapa*. Chronicle Books.

Gauvain, M. (2001). *The social context of cognitive development*. Guilford Press.

Gauvain, M. (2013). Sociocultural contexts of development. In P. D. Zelazo (Ed.), *Oxford handbook of developmental psychology* (Vol. 2; pp. 425–451). Oxford University Press.

Gender Spectrum. (n.d.). https://www.genderspectrum.org/

Gilbert, P. (2015). *Compassion: Universally misunderstood*. Huffington Post. https://www.huffingtonpost.co.uk/professor-paul-gilbert-obe/compassion-universally-misunderstood_b_8028276.html

Greater Good Science Center. (n.d.). *Empathy: Defined*. https://greatergood.berkeley.edu/topic/empathy/definition

Green, E. L. (2023, January 1). Strife in the schools: Education dept. logs record number of discrimination complaints. *The New York Times*. https://www.nytimes.com/2023/01/01/us/politics/education-discrimination.html?smid=nytcore-ios-share&referringSource=articleShare

Greenwald, A. G., Rudman, L. A., Nosek, B. A., Banaji, M. R., Farnham, S. D., & Mellot, D. S. (2002). A unified theory of implicit attitudes, stereotypes, self-esteem, and self-concept. *Psychological Review, 109*(1), 3–25.

Gullo, L. G., Capatosto, K., & Staats, C. (2018). *Implicit bias in schools: A practitioner's guide*. Routledge.

Gutiérrez, K. D., & Correa-Chavez, M. (2006). What to do about culture? *Lifelong Learning in Europe, 3*, 152–159.

Gutiérrez, K. D., & Rogoff, B. (2003). Cultural ways of learning: Individual traits or repertoires of practice. *Educational Researcher, 34*(5), 19–25. https://doi.org/10.3102/0013189X032005019

Hardy, K. (2013). Healing the wounds of racial trauma. *Reclaiming Children and Youth, 22*(1), 24–28.

Haynes, J., & Zacarian, D. (2010). *Teaching English language learners across the content areas*. ASCD.

Heineke, A. J., & Vera, E. M. (2022). Beyond language and academics: Investigating teachers' preparation to promote the social-emotional well-being of emergent bilingual learners. *Journal of Teacher Education, 73*(2), 145–158. https://doi.org/10.1177/00224871211027573

Hofstede, G. (2011). Dimensionalizing cultures: The Hofstede model in context. *Online Readings in Psychology* and Culture, *2*(1). https://doi.org/10.9707/2307-0919.1014

Hofstede, G., Hofstede, G. J., & Minkov, M. (2005). *Cultures and organizations: Software of the mind* (3rd ed.). McGraw Hill.

Hollins, E. R., & Guzman, M. T. (2005). Research on preparing teachers for diverse populations. In M. Cochran-Smith & K. M. Zeichner (Eds.), *Studying teacher education: The report of the AERA Panel on Research and Teacher Education* (pp. 477–548). Lawrence Erlbaum Associates Publishers and American Educational Research Association.

Howansky, K., Maimon, M., & Sanchez, D. (2021). Identity safety cues predict instructor impressions, belonging, and absences in the psychology classroom. *Society for the Teaching of Psychology, 49*(3), 212–217. https://doi:10.1177/0098628321990362

Howard, G. (1999). *We can't teach what we don't know: White teachers in multiracial schools*. Teachers College Press.

HRC Staff. (2019, May 31). *Stonewall at 50: Remembering importance of riots, pride and visibility*. Human Rights Campaign. https://www.hrc.org/news/stonewall-at-50-remembering-importance-of-riots-pride-and-visibility

Husband, T. (2012). "I don't see color": Challenging assumptions about discussing race with young children. *Early Childhood Education Journal, 39*(6), 365–371.

Iacurci, G. (2022, May 19). *Women are still paid 83 cents for every dollar men earn. Here's why*. CNBC https://www.cnbc.com/2022/05/19/women-are-still-paid-83-cents-for-every-dollar-men-earn-heres-why.html

Irwin, C. (2020). Say it loud—I'm Black, and I'm proud. VCR Classic Rock. https://ultimateclassicrock.com/james-brown-say-it-loud-im-black-and-im-proud/?utm_source=tsmclip&utm_medium=referral

Jha, S. (2016, August 9). *Dear Pope, don't transgender children deserve your love too?* Huffington Post. https://www.huffpost.com/entry/dear-pope-dont-transgender-children-deserve-your_b_57aa8e2fe4b091a07ef81110

Jha, S. (2018). *Read this, save lives: A teacher's guide to creating safe classrooms for LGBTQ+ students*. The Empathy Alliance.

Johnson, D. W., & Johnson, R. T. (2010). Cooperative learning and conflict resolution skills: Essential 21st-century skills. In J. Bellanca & R. Brandt (Eds.), *21st century skills: Rethinking how students learn* (pp. 201–220). Solution Tree Press.

Jones, N., Marks, R., Ramirez, R., & Rios-Vargas, M. (2021, August 12). *2020 Census illuminates racial and ethnic composition of the country*. U.S. Census Bureau. https://www.census.gov/library/stories/2021/08/improved-race-ethnicity-measures-reveal-united-states-population-much-more-multiracial.html

Jordan, M. (August 12, 2022). 'We Can't Claim Mission Accomplished': A Long Road for Afghan Refugees. *The New York Times*. https://www.nytimes.com/2022/08/12/us/afghanistan-refugees.html

Kahn, K. (2020, May 29). *Try to see me*. My Jewish Learning. https://www.myjewishlearning.com/2020/05/29/try-to-see-me/?_ga=2.24182009.234344980.1672352387-448578428.1672352387

Kallick, B., and Zmuda, A. (2017). *Students at the center: Personalizing learning and habits of mind*. ASCD.

Kawakami, N., & Miura, E. (2014). Effects of self-control resources on the interplay between implicit and explicit attitude processes in the subliminal mere exposure paradigm. *International Journal of Psychological Studies, 6*(2), 98–106.

Kendi, I. X. (2019). *How to be an antiracist*. Random House.

Krishnakumar, P. (2021, April 15). *This record-breaking year for anti-transgender legislation would affect minors the most.* CNN Politics. https://www.cnn.com /2021/04/15/politics/anti-transgender-legislation-2021/index.html

Ladson-Billings, G. (1994). *The Dreamkeepers: Successful teachers of African American children.* Jossey Bass.

Ladson-Billings, G. (1995). But that's just good teaching! The case for culturally relevant pedagogy. *Theory Into Practice, 34*(3), 159–165.

Lerner, R. M., Almerigi, J. B., Theokas, C., & Lerner, J. V. (2005). Positive youth development: A view of the issues. *Journal of Early Adolescence, 25*(1), 10–16.

Levin, B., Venolia, A., Perst, K., & Levin, B. (2022). *Report to the nation: 2020s— Dawn of a decade of rising hate.* Center for the Study of Hate and Extremism. California State University–San Bernardino.

Levine, P., & Kline, M. (2008) *Trauma-proofing your kids: A parent's guide for instilling confidence, joy, and resilience.* North Atlantic Books.

Lewis, A. E. (2003). *Race in the schoolyard: Negotiating the color line in classrooms and communities.* Rutgers University Press.

Little, B. (2018). *How boarding schools tried to 'kill the Indian' through assimilation: Native American tribes are still seeking the return of their children.* The History Channel. https://www.history.com/news/how-boarding-schools-tried-to-kill -the-indian-through-assimilation

Markus, H. R., Steele, C. M., & Steele D. M. (2000). Colorblindness as a barrier to inclusion: Assimilation and nonimmigrant minorities. *Daedalus, 129*(4), 233–259. https://www.jstor.org/stable/20027672

Maslow, A. (1999). *Toward a psychology of being* (3rd ed). John Wiley & Sons.

Maya, P. M.L. & Hames-García, M. (2000). *Reclaiming identity: Realist theory and the predicament of postmodernism.* University of California Press.

Merriam-Webster. (n.d.). Pride. In *Merriam-Webster.com dictionary.* Retrieved from https://www.merriam-webster.com/dictionary/pride

Moll, L. C., Amanti, C., Neff, D., & Gonzalez, N. (1992). Funds of knowledge for Teaching: Using a qualitative approach to connect homes and classrooms. *Theory Into Practice, 31*(2), 132–141. http://www.jstor.org/stable/1476399

Moll, L., Amanti, C., Neff, D., & González, N. (2005). Funds of knowledge for teaching: Using a qualitative approach to connect homes and classrooms. In N. Gonzalez, L. C. Moll, & C. Amanti (Eds.), *Funds of knowledge: Theorizing practices in households, communities, and classrooms* (pp. 83–100). Routledge.

Najarro, I. (2022). *With their licenses in jeopardy, Florida teachers unsure how the 'don't say gay' law will be applied.* Education Week. https://www.edweek .org/teaching-learning/with-their-licenses-in-jeopardy-florida-teachers -unsure-how-the-dont-say-gay-law-will-be-applied/2022/10

National Academies of Sciences, Engineering, and Medicine. (2022). *The impact of juvenile justice system involvement on the health and well-being of youth, families, and communities of color: Proceedings of a workshop.* The National Academies Press. https://doi.org/10.17226/26623.

National Center for Education Statistics [NCES]. (2018, May). Characteristics of public-school teachers. In *Condition of Education*. U.S. Department of Education. Institute of Education Sciences. https://nces.ed.gov/programs/coe/indicator/clr

National Center for Education Statistics [NCES]. (2020). Characteristics of postsecondary faculty. In *The Condition of Education 2020*. U.S. Department of Education. https://nces.ed.gov/programs/coe/pdf/coe_csc.pdf

National Education Association. (2022, August 28). *What educators should know about LGBTQ+ rights*. https://www.nea.org/resource-library/what-educators-should-know-about-lgbtq-rights

National Survey of Children's Health. (2016–17). Adverse childhood experiences, Nationwide. https://www.nschdata.org/browse/survey/results?q=5545&r=1

Neff, K. (2012). The power of self-compassion. *Greater Good Magazine.* https://greatergood.berkeley.edu/article/item/the_power_of_self_compassion

New York State Department of Education. (2022, August). *NYSESLAT—Determining an English Language Learner's (ELL) English language proficiency level.* https://www.nysed.gov/sites/default/files/programs/state-assessment/memo-nyseslat-conversion-charts-2022.pdf

Nieto, S. (1998). Affirmation, solidarity, and critique: Moving beyond tolerance. In E. Lee, D. Menkart, & M. Okazawa-Rey (Eds.), *Beyond heroes and holidays: A practical guide to K–12 anti-racist, multicultural education and staff development* (pp. 7–18). Teaching for Change.

Nieto, S. (1999). *The light in their eyes: Creating multicultural learning communities.* Teachers College Press.

O'Dell, C. (2008) *"The Churkendoose": Added to the national registry* [Essay]. The Library of Congress. https://www.loc.gov/static/programs/national-recording-preservation-board/documents/CHURKENDOOSE.pdf

Okeowo, A. (2016, November 17). Hate on the rise after Trump's election, *The New Yorker*. https://www.newyorker.com/news/news-desk/hate-on-the-rise-after-trumps-election

PEN America, (2022). *Educational gag orders: Legislative restrictions on the freedom to read, learn, and teach.* PEN America Report. https://pen.org/wp-content/uploads/2022/02/PEN_EducationalGagOrders_01-18-22-compressed.pdf

Phinney, J. (1990). Ethnic identity in adolescents and adults: Review of research. *Psychological Bulletin, 108*(3), 499–514.

Pompei, V. (2022). Responding to pushback. *ACSA School Counselor.* American School Counselor Association.

powell, j. (n.d.) *Our story.* Othering & Belonging Institute. https://belonging.berkeley.edu/our-story

Purdie-Vaughns, V., Steele, C. M., Davies, P. G., Ditlmann, R., & Crosby, J. R. (2008). Social identity contingencies: How diversity cues signal threat or safety for African Americans in mainstream institutions. *Journal of Personality and Social Psychology, 94*(4): 615–630. https://doi.org/10.1037/0022-3514.94.4.615

Quinn, E. (2018). *The way we think about biological sex is wrong* [Video]. TED-Women. https://www.ted.com/talks/emily_quinn_the_way_we_think_about_biological_sex_is_wrong/transcript?language=en

Quintero, D., & Hansen, M. (2021, January 14). *As we tackle school segregation, don't forget about English learner students*. Brookings Institution. https://www.brookings.edu/blog/brown-center-chalkboard/2021/01/14/as-we-tackle-school-segregation-dont-forget-about-english-learner-students

Robles de Mélendez, W., & Beck, V. (2019). *Teaching young children in multicultural classrooms: Issues, concepts, and strategies* (5th ed.) Cengage Learning.

Ryan, C., Russell, S. T., Huebner, D., Diaz, R., & Sanchez, J. (2010). Family acceptance in adolescence and the health of LGBT young adults. *Journal of Child and Adolescent Psychiatric Nursing, 23*(4), 205–213. https://doi.org/10.1111/j.1744-6171.2010.00246.x

Samson, J. F., & Lesaux, N. K. (2015). Disadvantaged language minority students and their teachers: A national picture. *Teachers College Record, 117*(2), 1–26. https://doi.org/10.1177/016146811511700205

Sawchuk, S. (2021, May 18). *What is critical race theory and why is it under attack?* Education Week. https://www.edweek.org/leadership/what-is-critical-race-theory-and-why-is-it-under-attack/2021/05

Shanker, S. (2016). *Self-reg: How to help your child (and you) break the stress cycle and successfully engage with life*. Penguin Press.

Solomon, A. (2012). *Far from the tree: Parents, children, and the search for identity*. Scribner.

Southern Education Foundation. (2015). *New majority series*. https://southerneducation.org/what-we-do/research-and-policy/newmajorityreportseries/

Spencer, S. J., Logel, C., & Davies, P. G. (2016). Stereotype threat. *Annual Review of Psychology, 67*(1), 415–437.

Steele, C. M. (1997). A threat in the air: How stereotypes shape intellectual identity and performance. *American Psychologist, 52*(6), 613–629. https://doi.org/10.1037/0003-066X.52.6.613

Steele, C. M. (1999). Thin ice: "Stereotype threat" and Black college students. *The Atlantic Monthly, 284*(2), 44–47, 50–54. https://www.theatlantic.com/magazine/archive/1999/08/thin-ice-stereotype-threat-and-black-college-students/304663/

Steele, C. M. (2011). *Whistling Vivaldi: How stereotypes affect us and what we can do*. W. W. Norton & Company.

Steele, C. M., & Aronson, J. (1995). Stereotype threat and the intellectual test performance of African Americans. *Journal of Personality and Social Psychology, 69*(5), 797–811.

Steele, D. M. (2012). Creating identity safe classrooms. In J. A. Banks (Ed.) *Encyclopedia of diversity in education* (Vol. 1; pp. 1125–1128). Sage.

Steele, D. M., & Cohn-Vargas, B. (2013). *Identity safe classrooms, K–5: Places to belong and learn*. Corwin.

Steinpreis, R., Anders, K. A., & Ritzke, D. (1999). The impact of gender on the review of the curricula vitae of job applicants and tenure candidates: A national empirical study. *Sex Roles, 41*(7/8), 509–528. https://doi.org/10.1023/A:1018839203698

Stern, M. J. (2022, March 2). *How the war on critical race theory revived anti-gay activism in schools.* Slate. https://slate.com/news-and-politics/2022/03/critical-race-theory-dont-say-gay-florida-lgbtq.html

Stevenson, A. (Ed.). (2015). Upstander. In *Oxford Dictionary of English,* Online version. (3rd ed.) Oxford University Press. https://www.oxfordreference.com/display/10.1093/acref/9780199571123.001.0001/m_en_gb1009527;jsessionid=856579A613B061C026A4F42102026B8F

Sullivan, J. (2020, August 27). *Children notice race several years before adults want to talk about it.* American Psychological Association. https://www.apa.org/news/press/releases/2020/08/children-notice-race

Tatum, B. D. (1997). *Why are all the Black kids sitting together in the cafeteria?* Basic Books.

Taylor, R. D., Oberle, E., Durlak, J. A., & Weissberg, R. P. (2017). Promoting positive youth development through school-based social and emotional learning interventions: A meta-analysis of follow-up effects. *Child Development, 88*(4), 1156–1171. https://doi.org/10.1111/cdev.12864

The Trevor Project. (2022). *2022 National survey on LGBTQ youth mental health.* https://www.thetrevorproject.org/survey-2022/#

Trueba, H., Guthrie, G. P., & Au, K. H. (1981). *Culture and the classroom: Studies in classroom ethnography.* Newbury House.

Tyler, K. M., Uqdah, A. L., Dillihunt, M. L., Beatty-Hazelbaker, R., Conner, T., Gadson, N. C., Henchy, A. M., Hughes, T., Mulder, S., Owens, E., Roan-Belle, C., Smith, L., & Stevens, R. (2008). Cultural discontinuity: Toward the quantitative investigation of a major hypothesis in education. *Educational Researcher, 37*(5), 280–297. https://doi.org/10.3102/0013189X08321459

U.S. Department of Education (n.d.-a). *About IDEA.* https://sites.ed.gov/idea/about-idea

U.S. Department of Education (n.d.-b). *Every Student Succeeds Act* (ESSA). https://www.ed.gov/essa?src=rn

U.S. Department of Education. (n.d.-c). *Our nation's English learners: What are their characteristics?* https://www2.ed.gov/datastory/el-characteristics/index.html

U.S. Department of Education. (n.d.-d). Title IX NPRM summary of major provisions chart. https://www2.ed.gov/about/offices/list/ocr/docs/t9nprm-chart.pdf

U.S. Department of Education. (2020). *Developing programs for English language learners: Plan development.* https://www2.ed.gov/about/offices/list/ocr/ell/plandev.html

U.S. Department of Education. (2021). *U.S. Department of Education confirms Title IX protects students from discrimination based on sexual orientation and gender identity.* https://www.ed.gov/news/press-releases/us-department-education-confirms-title-ix-protects-students-discrimination-based-sexual-orientation-and-gender-identity

U.S. Department of Education. (2022). *U.S. Department of Education's 2022 proposed amendments to its Title IX regulations* [Fact sheet]. https://www2.ed.gov/about/offices/list/ocr/docs/t9nprm-factsheet.pdf

U.S. Department of Justice and U.S. Department of Education. (2015, January 7). https://www2.ed.gov/ocr/letters/colleague-el-201501.pdf

Van Ausdale, D., & Feagan, J. R. (2001). *The first R: How children learn race and racism.* Rowan & Littlefield.

Vargas, C. (2016). *Dr. Clemencia Vargas: The goals of dental screening* [Video]. ¡Colorín Colorado!. https://www.colorincolorado.org/video/dr-clemencia-vargas

Vygotsky, L. (1978*). Mind in society* (M. Cole, Trans.). Harvard University Press.

Winerman, L. (2005). The mind's mirror. *Monitor on Psychology, 36*(9), 48. https://www.apa.org/monitor/oct05/mirror

Zacarian, D. (2013). *Mastering academic language: A framework for supporting student achievement.* Corwin Press.

Zacarian, D. (2023). *Transforming schools for multilingual learners: A comprehensive guide for educators* (2nd Ed.). Corwin.

Zacarian, D., Alvarez-Ortiz, L., & Haynes, J. (2017). *Teaching to strengths: Supporting students living with trauma, violence, and chronic stress.* ASCD.

Zacarian, D., Calderón, M. E., & Gottlieb, M. (2021). *Beyond crises: Overcoming linguistic and cultural inequities in communities, schools, and classrooms.* Corwin.

Zacarian, D. & Cohn-Vargas, B. (2020, June 11). As schools reopen, a new inclusive paradigm is needed. *Norton Education K–12 Talk.* https://k-12talk.com/2020/06/11/as-schools-reopen-a-new-inclusive-paradigm-is-needed/

Zacarian, D., & Dove, M. (2020*).* From nobody cares to everyone/every community cares. In M. Espino Calderón, M. G. Dove, D. Staehr Fenner, M. Gottlieb, A. Honigsfeld, T. W. Singer, S. Slakk, I. Soto, & D. Zacarian (Eds.), *Breaking down the wall: Essential shifts for English learners' success* (pp. 187–199). Corwin.

Zacarian, D., & Silverstone, M. A. (2015*). In it together: How student, family, and community partnerships advance engagement and achievement in diverse classrooms.* Corwin.

Zacarian, D., & Silverstone, M. A. (2020). *Teaching to empower: Taking action to foster student agency, self-confidence, and collaboration.* ASCD.

Zacarian D., & Soto, I. (2020). *Responsive schooling for culturally and linguistically diverse students.* Norton Education.

Zacarian, D., & Staehr Fenner, D, M. (2020*). From deficits-based to assets-based.* In M. Espino Calderón, M. G. Dove, D. Staehr Fenner, M. Gottlieb, A. Honigsfeld, T. W. Singer, S. Slakk, I. Soto, & D. Zacarian (Eds.). *Breaking down the wall: Essential shifts for English learners' success* (pp. 1–20). Corwin.

Index

About the Authors

Becki Cohn-Vargas is a consultant and curriculum specialist who provides professional development and expertise on topics of identity safety, culturally responsive teaching, and bullying prevention. Becki coauthored the best-selling book *Identity Safe Classrooms K–5: Places to Belong and Learn*. Subsequently, she coauthored *Identity Safe Classrooms Grades 6–12: Pathways to Belonging and Learning* and *Belonging and Inclusion in Identity Safe Schools: A Guide for Educational Leaders*. In addition, she has published book chapters and numerous articles. She has produced films and curriculum guides, including *Our Family, A Film About Family Diversity* and the *Guide to Bullying Prevention for Law Enforcement* for the U.S. Department of Justice. Becki was hosted twice at the White House by President Obama's education staff and has worked as a consultant in over 150 schools across the United States. She spent over 35 years as a Spanish bilingual teacher, principal, curriculum director, and superintendent in pre-K–12 rural, urban, and suburban school districts, where she focused on fostering educational equity.

Debbie Zacarian delivers professional development and policy advocacy tailored to PreK–university educators serving culturally and linguistically diverse populations. She is the author/coauthor of numerous national and state language education policies in conjunction with governmental bodies and educational institutions, including the Massachusetts Parent Information Resource Center, Departments of Early Education and Care and Elementary and Secondary Education, and Federation for Children with Special Needs. Debbie served on the faculty of the University of Massachusetts–Amherst. Her professional journey also includes being a program director at the Collaborative for Educational Services, where she spearheaded professional development benefiting thousands of educators and strategic consulting and policy evaluation on behalf of numerous educational institutions.

A pioneering figure in language education, she was the founding director of the Amherst Public Schools' programming for bi-multilingual learners, achieving noteworthy commendations at the local, state, and national levels. With a master's degree in clinical psychology and doctorate in educational policy and research, Debbie boasts an impressive literary portfolio encompassing several bestselling and highly acclaimed professional publications.

Printed and bound by CPI Group (UK) Ltd, Croydon, CR0 4YY

09/06/2025

14685968-0001